HOW AM I
SMART?

HOW AM I SMART?

A PARENT'S GUIDE TO MULTIPLE INTELLIGENCES

DR. KATHY KOCH

MOODY PUBLISHERS
CHICAGO

Scripture taken from the *Holy Bible, New International Version*®. NIV®. Copyright ©
1973, 1978, 1984 by International Bible Society. Used by permission of Zondervan.
All rights reserved.

Cover Design: Tim Green / The DesignWorks Group (www.thedesignworksgroup.com)
Cover Imagery: Getty Images, Gandee Vasan
Interior Design: Smartt Guys design
Editor: Diane Eble

Library of Congress Cataloging-in-Publication Data

Koch, Kathy.
    How am I smart? : a parent's guide to multiple intelligences / Kathy Koch.
        p. cm.
    Includes bibliographical references and index.
    ISBN-13: 978-0-8024-0283-7
    ISBN-10: 0-8024-0283-6
    1. Multiple intelligences—Religious aspects—Christianity. 2. Intellect—
Religious aspects—Christianity. 3. Multiple intelligences. I. Title.

BV4509.5.K64 2007
153.9--dc22

                                                                    2006038863

We hope you enjoy this book from Moody Publishers. Our goal is to provide high-
quality, thought-provoking books and products that connect truth to your real needs
and challenges. For more information on other books and products written and pro-
duced from a biblical perspective, go to www.moodypublishers.com or write to:

Moody Publishers
820 N. LaSalle Boulevard
Chicago, IL 60610

1 3 5 7 9 10 8 6 4 2

Printed in the United States of America

I dedicate How Am I Smart? *to Jesus,*
the Master Teacher, and my Savior and Lord.
Although His teaching ministry didn't last long,
it has had a long impact.
It will continue for eternity.
Jesus Christ was often called Teacher.
He was never called preacher, church planter,
evangelist, or carpenter.

I'm grateful for the emphasis the Master Teacher placed on Truth.
I'm also thankful for His teaching abilities, passions, and priorities.
He taught for understanding and application.
He is my Role Model Teacher.
I believe He taught well to all the smarts.
May we do the same!

CONTENTS

ACKNOWLEDGMENTS

I'm grateful for God's presence in my life, as Father, Son, and Holy Spirit. I praise Him for saving me, meeting my needs, and equipping and empowering me to love, obey, serve, write, and teach.

I treasure my mom's love and support. She is significant to me! She and my dad raised me well and taught me to believe in myself. I'm grateful to them both. I'm also proud of my mom for fully embracing life after my dad's death. She inspires me.

Celebrate Kids, Inc., board members have been totally supportive for years. Robert Adams, Mark Davis, Andrea Heitz, Ron Horton, and Timmie Mosley are important to me. Without their support and belief, I could not have written this book.

I can easily say the same thing about my staff. They are multitalented, joyful, focused, and very supportive. Marilyn Birdwell, Marie Collins, Denice Crawford, Sandra Critz, Linda Depler, Rolando Ford, Sandi Fowler, Karen Fuller, Tina Hollenbeck, Nancy Matheis, Sharon May, Miki Michaelsen, Joyce Penninger, Rachelle Riley, Maya Smith, and Jeanie Taylor are God's gifts to me. Mike Penninger, Jr., our information technologist, has also served me well.

Chip Griepsma and my mom both allowed me to stay with them for several weeks so I could get more writing accomplished. This practical support blessed me. My mom, Chip Griepsma, Linda Page, and Tina Hollenbeck reacted to drafts of several sections and offered helpful suggestions. Others, including Brian Ziemer, Billie McConnell, Brad Sargent, Debbie Koch, JK Williams, and Melanie Ligocki, helped me think through some specific sections. I'm especially indebted to Sarah Carpenter who used her picture-smart and people-smart strengths to help me come up with the interest and ability graphs used to rate the smarts. I'm grateful! I'm also thankful for the family members and friends who allowed me to tell their stories within these pages. I appreciate their trust.

As with my first book, I'm pleased to be a part of the Moody Publishers family. Peg Short was always encouraging and clear. Diane Eble was also positive and professional. Her suggestions strengthened the book. The enthusiasm of Janis Backing, Rhonda Elfstrand, and Lori Wenzinger to publicize and market this book encourages me. I didn't write it just to write it. I want it read and I pray the information and ideas truly help parents, children, and educators. I know everyone at Moody wants the same thing.

PREFACE

Too many children ask, "Am *I* smart?" and "How smart *am* I?" The better question is, "*How* am I smart?" God has uniquely created all children with a combination of intelligences: They may be *word* smart, *logic* smart, *picture* smart, *music* smart, *body* smart, *nature* smart, *people* smart, and *self* smart. You are privileged to help children identify which ones are their strengths, which can be improved upon, and which still need to be awakened. Inspiring children to believe they are smart in many ways is exhilarating. Doubts lift. Excuses fade away. Now they know they can be successful in school and in life.

From reading this book, you'll not only be able to discern your children's strongest and weakest intelligences, you'll be able to convince them they are smart. You'll uncover how they can learn and study with all eight intelligences and how their misbehavior might be connected to their strengths. You'll gain valuable insights into your relationships and your occasional struggles.

Wherever you are currently regarding your children's education —home, private, Christian, or public school, not yet in school, or already out of school—you'll find much valuable information for both you and your children. You'll also be empowered to share insights about your children with their teachers so they can more effectively support them.

Get ready to dig, because there's lots of precious ore in this gold mine! I pray you find many, many golden nuggets that brighten the days and years ahead. As a result, I trust you'll celebrate your children even more than you currently do.

May your children be smart with their smarts! To God be the glory!

"HOW AM I SMART?"

AN INTRODUCTION TO MULTIPLE INTELLIGENCES

Grace[1] and Melody, two young girls I know well, are into princesses and ballet. Grace and Melody love their ballet class and often dance through their home to the music playing in their minds. They prefer wearing dresses because that's what princesses and ballerinas wear. Plus, they like the way they look when twirling around as they dance.

Their mom, Anna, and I have joked that Grace and Melody, even though they're only three and four years old, could win a trivia game about Disney princesses and the Barbie videos, if anyone ever created such a game. They watch and rewatch the videos, have memorized some of the dialogue, and often pretend they're Cinderella, Ariel, Odette, or Elina.

God used these quality videos to awaken at least three of

Melody's and Grace's eight intelligences—or "smarts"—their music smart, picture smart, and body smart. What do I mean?

Many of the videos the girls watch, like the Barbie versions of the *Nutcracker* and *Swan Lake*, include gorgeous classical music recorded by some of the best orchestras in the world. At a very young age, as they've heard numerous instruments in stunning combinations, their music-smart intelligences have been awakened.

The videos are visually appealing. These fast-moving productions have exposed the girls to vivid colors, stimulated their creativity and imaginations, and sparked their picture-smart intelligences.

Melody and Grace observe the characters dancing in the videos, so they dance. From twirling and leaping throughout the living room, they gain balance and an understanding of how their bodies work. This movement activates their body-smart intelligences.

Melody and Grace's parents haven't left it at that, though. They parent the way I hope you do! They respond to the girls' obvious interests in dance and music. As a result, their girls' music, body, and picture smarts weren't merely awakened, they have been strengthened and, more significantly, trained.

In addition to the videos, the development of these girls' music smart is influenced by their mom's playing worship CDs in their home. The girls attend a church that has a vibrant worship program, so they're exposed to music there, too. Because Anna is part of the worship team, her daughters hear her practicing her singing parts, and occasionally her oboe and saxophone. There's a piano in their living room, and the girls know they will take piano lessons when they're older. I just had dinner at their house and we sang the prayer! Music abounds in their home and is important to Anna and her husband, Will.

Grace's and Melody's picture-smart abilities have been further activated with the blank paper, crayons, and many creative coloring books that Anna and Will purchase for them. What do the girls draw? Dancing princesses, of course! As Melody and Grace grow older and gain additional eye-hand coordination, their picture-smart abilities will continue to improve. The point is to start with expressed interests. These girls have lots of interest in activities that grow their picture smarts!

To help strengthen Melody's and Grace's body smarts, Anna and Will chose to enroll them in a dance class. That wise decision honored the girls' strong interest in ballet, which stemmed from their video viewing. Once a week they attend class with several other little girls. Their balance and coordination is improving. The girls learn special dance positions and steps and are enjoying dancing more and more.

I was privileged to attend Melody and Grace's first dance recital. They looked adorable in their bright lime tutus with puffy velvet sleeves. Just like the other girls in the group, they stared at the audience during part of the dance, looked at the girls next to them for a while, and then managed to dance a few steps. They were perfect for beginners. At home, Grace and Melody love wearing their tutus as they dance throughout the house. They look forward to continuing their lessons.

Some teens at Melody and Grace's recital have clearly chosen to focus on dance. They've taken lessons for years and their body-smart and music-smart intelligences have been focused and trained. They are quite talented. One dancer, in particular, impressed me. I believe she had more music-smart abilities than the other dancers. Though the other girls danced to the beat, I sensed she actually *felt* the music. She interpreted the emotion in the songs through her facial expressions and the flow of her arms. Our eight intelligences rarely, if ever, work alone, and this is a beautiful example of that. Her music-smartness enhanced the way she used her body-smart abilities.

Melody and Grace have been in their dancing and princess phases for a long time. Eventually other things will interest them. They may leave dancing and princesses totally behind, or these interests may continue while other interests develop. Some children tend to focus; others broaden their interests. There's probably nothing wrong with either approach, as long as children are content and pursuing their own dreams and not their parents'.

Maybe your children are into soccer, video games, math, or reading. It's important that we expose young children to a variety of activities so their own unique, God-designed passions can be discovered. Considerate parents nurture their development.

WHAT ARE THE
MULTIPLE INTELLIGENCES?

Dr. Howard Gardner, of Harvard University, is considered the father of the theory of multiple intelligences. His first book on this topic was published in 1983. Others, including his former colleague, Dr. Tom Armstrong, have written more popularized and less academic versions of Dr. Gardner's work. For example, in the chart that follows, you can see that Dr. Armstrong's labels for the intelligences are easier to understand. Therefore, I'll use them in this book.

THE EIGHT INTELLIGENCES

Dr. Armstrong's Labels	Dr. Gardner's Labels
Word smart	Linguistic intelligence
Logic smart	Logical-Mathematical intelligence
Picture smart	Spatial intelligence
Music smart	Musical intelligence
Body smart	Bodily-Kinesthetic intelligence
Nature smart	Naturalist intelligence
People smart	Interpersonal intelligence
Self smart	Intrapersonal intelligence

Dr. Gardner determined that everyone is born with all eight of these distinct intelligences.[2] Each intelligence has to be awakened, but they're there, built into each child at birth. I like to use the words *nature* (the genetic makeup we inherited from our parents) and *nurture* (the varied experiences and attitudes that influence our development), when teaching about the source of our intelligences. *God has "wired" everyone with eight intelligences.* He created our unique combination of genes and wants us to develop His gift of the varied intelligences. Dr. Gardner stated the idea this way, "I reject the 'inherited versus learned' dichotomy and instead stress the interaction, from the moment of conception, between genetic and environmental factors."[3]

Unfortunately, because of sin entering the world, some children's intelligences aren't developed. Perhaps illness or disease is the cause. For example, Merry, the twenty-one-year-old daughter of our scheduling director, is both physically and mentally severely disabled, with capabilities similar to a two-month-old. Yet Miki beams when sharing evidence that Merry's strongest intelligences are music and people. The nurturing Merry receives from her parents, younger sister, teachers, caregivers, and family friends makes the difference. Though the development is very limited, Merry responds to music and people around her. For instance, when a prospective nurse arrives, Merry's parents have learned to use Merry's quick evaluation when determining whether to hire her. Merry will give her mom a certain look if she doesn't like the nurse, and Miki knows not to hire her.

A lack of quality nurturing experiences and attitudes can also stunt the development of a child's intelligences. If a child grows up with apathetic or absent parents, poverty, abuse, or any number of other factors that lead to poor parenting, his or her intelligences may remain dormant throughout life.

When you help nurture your children's smarts, as Merry's parents have done, you cooperate with God in the development of your child's full potential. Nature and nurture together determine which intelligences will become strengths, which ones may not develop much at all, and which ones will plateau at a point in between.

The earlier we awaken children's smarts, the greater the likelihood they might be developed as strengths. Don't get me wrong—it's never too late to awaken a part of the mind. A particular intelligence might not become a definite strength because of a late start, but any smart can be improved, focused, and trained. Moreover, once it's awakened and stretched, it never goes back to its original size. Picture a balloon. You can always tell if it's been used. The mind is the same. I'm a former viola player, so I could more easily learn to play that instrument again in less time than someone who has never played it. Perhaps you can think of an example of this "it's never too late" principle from your life.

We don't rely on just one smart at any one time. For example, when using word smart to read, many people will use their logic smart to ask questions about what they're reading. They may also use their picture smart to create visual images of what they're reading. Playing chess uses the picture-smart and logic-smart intelligences. If you're playing golf, you'd add body smart to those two, and perhaps nature smart, too.

Even though our smarts always work together, for the purposes of this book, I'll be writing about "music-smart children" and "people-smart children," etc. This doesn't mean these children[4] don't have the other seven intelligences. It's just that I need to isolate the qualities of each in order for you to understand them.

HOW CAN UNDERSTANDING MULTIPLE INTELLIGENCES HELP CHILDREN?

Your children probably wonder if they're smart. (If you're typical, you've wondered if you're smart, too!) If your children haven't asked, "Am I smart?" have they ever asked, "How smart am I?" Are your children ever discouraged because they don't think they're as smart as they need to be? Perhaps you're sometimes disheartened, too.

One of the main reasons to learn about the eight intelligences is to discover *how* your children are smart. Such practical knowledge about the unique ways God designed each of us should encourage, inspire, and empower you, as well as your children. The question changes from being about the amount of their intelligence ("How smart am I?") to which intelligences they have ("How am I smart?") and how they will use them ("How can I be smart with my smarts?")

An understanding of the intelligences can lead to an improvement in your children's grades. When they study with more than one intelligence, they're bound to better understand what they're learning. They'll remember what they learn longer, apply their learning more accurately, and possess more optimism for the future. Successes in applying the multiple intelligences will help reinforce the best question: "How am I smart?"

I enjoy helping children understand that they're smart in eight different ways: word, logic, picture, music, body, nature, people, and self. However, at the beginning of my school assemblies, some children have a hard time believing me. They truly doubt they're intelligent. Maybe school is hard for them. Or they may have been told they're stupid. Maybe they don't earn many A's. Something or someone has caused them to believe they're not smart.

As I describe each of these intelligences, they begin to believe the evidence I provide. They elbow their friends and I see them mouth the words, "That's me!" Healing of past hurts and current doubts often occurs. I rejoice when I see that. The children relax before my eyes. By the end of the program, when I ask them to raise their hands to indicate their top four intelligences, many struggle with the limit. What joy to see them go from not thinking they're smart to struggling to choose only four intelligence strengths an hour later!

It's also a delight to help children understand they can learn with all eight intelligences. They don't have to study everything with all eight, but they can learn to choose which intelligences to use with different activities and assignments. In addition, ideally their teachers will use a variety of intelligences while teaching. Of course, you can use different intelligences when helping your children complete their homework or study for tests. (Chapters three to ten are full of many ideas.)

Multiple intelligences don't just help children understand how they're smart in different ways. Intelligence strengths also help to explain why children might be prone to get into certain types of trouble. For example, picture-smart children like drawing and creating. Therefore, they might color on the report you wrote for your boss and left on the table. Logic-smart children like exploring things on their own, so they might walk away from you to go investigate something that catches their attention. When children understand the cause of the behavior that gets them into trouble, they are more empowered to change. You'll have more hope, too! Children may also be encouraged to discover that improving their behavior simply requires them to use their intelligences in different ways or with less intensity to help and not hurt themselves and others. They need to be smart with their smarts!

Recently, one of my coworkers heard me speak on this topic. As we talked on the drive back from the training event, she began to see her ten-year-old grandson in a new and very positive light. She realized the behaviors that often irritated his cousins, classmates, and teachers were rooted in his body-smart and logic-smart strengths. That night, she lovingly explained to him what she had learned and asked if he agreed with her that he was very body smart and logic smart. He lit up when discovering he was smart in these two important ways. At the office the next day, my coworker smiled broadly when testifying that her grandson was different that morning. Her summary comment says a lot: "It makes a difference to be understood, doesn't it?" Yes!

I teach children they can choose to be stupid, but God didn't make them that way. As that truth sinks in, they laugh. Being smart is a choice. So is stupidity. Children can choose to *not* use their intelligences, to let their strengths get them into trouble, or to use their smarts for evil purposes. Such choices, of course, are stupid.

I often teach young people that much of the evil in the world is done by smart people who are stupid. They get it, and nervous laughter follows. At one extreme are those who caused the tragedies on 9/11. Among other things, those men had to be logic smart to get through airport security with weapons, choose which airplanes to hijack, and get into the planes' cockpits. They were probably body smart, too, and used this intelligence for evil.

Admittedly, that's an extreme example of an unhealthy use of intelligences. The point is that we constantly make choices when using our intelligences. Throughout my school and church programs, I demonstrate that much of the trouble children get into is a result of using their strengths in improper or ill-timed ways. Children are not necessarily stupid and not necessarily "bad," but rather have not learned self-control, self-respect, and/or respect for others. These are keys to children (and adults) being able to use their intelligence strengths for good and not evil, to help and not hurt.

Does your son keep his eyes glued to his book when you've asked him to talk with his grandmother? He may be *word smart*.

Does your daughter struggle with obedience because she's always asking, "Why?" She may be *logic smart*. Does your daughter doodle all over her notes rather than studying her notes? She may be *picture smart*. Does your son irritate others with his constant humming and finger tapping? He may be *music smart*. Do your children constantly move and touch everything? They may be *body smart*. Does your daughter pay so much attention to her cats that she doesn't finish her homework? She may be *nature smart*. Does your son interrupt you constantly because he needs to know what you think about his ideas? He may be *people smart*. Does your daughter spend most of her time alone and ignore your input? She may be *self smart*.

Multiple intelligences are also worth understanding because God can use them to help meet our core needs. As I'll explain in the next chapter, God created us with a need for security, identity, belonging, purpose, and competence. Would you like your children to have healthy answers to the questions represented by these needs? *Who can I trust? Who am I? Who wants me? Why am I alive? What do I do well?* Knowing which intelligences are their strengths and how to use them in smart ways can help children meet these five basic needs. When needs are met, it's more likely they'll experience contentment, peace, and obedience.

HOW CAN I IDENTIFY MY CHILD'S MULTIPLE INTELLIGENCE STRENGTHS?

Within each intelligence, there's what I call a "hierarchy of giftedness." As I explained, each child's potential for the eight intelligences depends on nature and nurture. Yet we know they have all eight to some level. God may have designed your son's mind to have logic-smart strengths. You maybe haven't called them that before, but you will once you see him in the descriptions and details I include in the logic-smart chapter. Perhaps you noticed his natural leanings toward solving puzzles when he was young (i.e., his nature) and, therefore, you created relevant experiences for him (i.e., the nurture). Or, because of his interest, he created his own experiences and you had no choice but to go along with him! These experiences and interactions strengthened and focused this intelligence so that he may currently have a great deal of logic-smart ability.

At the same time, as you read the logic-smart chapter, it should be clear which of your children needs to have this intelligence awakened because it's very weak. You'll also see that other children's logic-smart abilities and interests may fall somewhere in the middle. As a result, you'll decide which activities and focused instruction you will encourage to strengthen their logic-smartness.

I'm not a fan of children comparing themselves to others. That's one reason I don't like the questions "Am I smart?" and "How smart am I?" Comparing causes some children to feel good about themselves and others to feel bad. Comparing encourages some parents to gloat about their children while other parents hope no one asks them about their children's abilities.

Some comparisons *are* healthy, however. For example, it can be very valuable for children to compare themselves to their former selves. I know they feel smarter at the end of my programs than at the beginning, and that's a good thing! When they make wise choices one day, I want them to know they're smarter than they were the day before. When they study with more than one intelligence, they're smarter than when they studied with just one.

An additional comparison is very important. I ask children to express it this way: *"God is smarter than I am!"* Smart children understand that God will always be smarter than they are. In addition, smart children know they need a smart God. I tell them that God could have created them to be like marionette puppets that He controls. Instead, He gave them eight different intelligences and He trusts them to use those smarts to help and not hurt. That's humbling, isn't it?

You must observe and know your children to discern which intelligences are strengths and which aren't. Spending time with your children—to see and to hear them—is essential. This will reveal their strengths and weaknesses, as well as answers to valuable questions like these: What's easy for them? What's hard for them? What do they avoid doing? What holds their attention? What do they do in their spare time? What do they play? How do they play? In what classes do they do well? In what classes do they consistently struggle? What gives them joy? What gets them into trouble? What about them drives me nuts?

Teaching children about the smarts can help you identify their intelligence strengths and weaknesses. You can observe their reactions to details and examples you share and note which ones pique their curiosity. Then ask *them* to identify their strengths. They'll often know and be able to provide evidence. Often it's also easy for them to indicate which of the smarts are their weakest. (As you'll understand after reading chapter ten, children who are not very self smart will have a harder time with this self-analysis.)

Each chapter that covers a particular intelligence ends with a graph like the one below. You'll place the names of your children in the correct quadrant by considering the information I present and what you know about your children. You'll do this for yourself, too. As you can see from the graph, you'll consider both ability and interest for each intelligence.

For example, in my music-smart sample on the next page for the Diff family:

- Latrice has been judged by her parents as having both *high ability* and *high interest.* She is apparently talented and enjoying using her musical abilities.
- On the other hand, Corey currently has *high interest*, but *low ability.* Even though he lacks ability, it's encouraging that he still has interest. If his ability doesn't improve, though, his interest may eventually wane. Therefore, his parents should intervene. Perhaps private lessons would help, or maybe his parents could help him take his practice times more seriously.
- Justin's situation is the opposite. He has plenty of *ability*, but *low interest.* His intervention needs to be different than Corey's. Maybe Justin's interest will increase when he's allowed to play different musical selections. Perhaps attending a professional concert, where he'll see and hear polished performers, will inspire him to commit, again, to his trombone.
- Her parents have judged Kelly as having *low interest* and *low ability.* She's only three, though, so there's no reason to worry. They're a bit surprised that she hasn't shown interest in the little songs that are a family tradition, but they're encouraged that her other intelligences seem to be developing well. They'll watch more carefully for the next month or two to

see if any particular musical style causes a reaction in Kelly. If so, they plan to use that to engage her mind. (If we were rating word smart or logic smart, which relate more directly to school success, I would encourage Kelly's parents to plan some nurturing experiences right away.)

- Both parents are most like Corey. They have *great interest*, but their *ability* isn't currently strong. (Perhaps when they were younger, they would have been judged to have high ability and high interest, but that's no longer the case.)

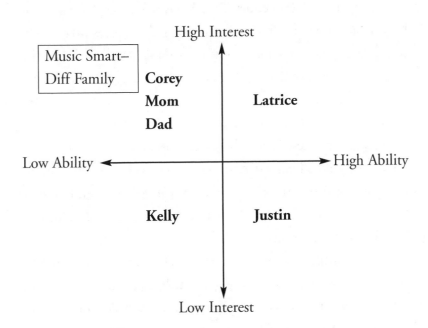

These graphs can also shed light on conflicts within your family. For instance, let's consider word smart. You and your oldest son might be in opposite quadrants. Perhaps by the end of that chapter you'll see that you have high ability and high interest, while your son has neither. Maybe this is why you become impatient when he cannot express himself as easily or clearly as you can.

Maybe by the end of the nature-smart chapter you'll see that your youngest daughter has high ability and high interest, while you don't have much of either. This difference can explain why you have a hard time deciding what to do together on Saturdays, why she collects pinecones and acorns even though you don't like the mess in her bedroom, and why she's so interested in cloud formations and you're not.

Awakening, strengthening, and training children's multiple intelligences are key ways to help them become who God created them uniquely to be. By discerning children's passions and potentials, and nurturing their development, you help them fulfill their God-given niche in the family, community, church, and in history. This is a significant responsibility!

The next brief chapter will explain children's five core needs, and why I've organized the eight intelligence chapters around them. I'll also introduce the very important concepts of paralysis and crystallization. You'll want to learn how to do one and how *not* to do the other!

WHAT ARE MY CORE NEEDS?

HOW ARE MULTIPLE INTELLIGENCES RELEVANT?

I have taught thousands of parents, teachers, children, and teens about their multiple intelligences. I never get tired of the looks on people's faces when I begin talking about a smart that's one of their greatest strengths. They sit up straighter and smile broader. Their eyebrows do what I commonly refer to as "the eyebrow lift" and their entire body relaxes. It's almost as if I can see their spirit soaking in the encouragement as they realize *they are smart*!

I'll also never tire of watching family members, teachers, students, and friends interact during my message. Parents and children elbow each other, smile, and point when one of my examples captures their strengths and relationship. Friends laugh, point, stare, and get serious all within minutes of each other as the content strikes them as true. Students glance toward their teachers when I say something relevant to their relationship or smart strengths. Teachers glance toward particular children when I explain that sometimes our strengths get us into trouble. When children recognize themselves in my illustrations, they return the glance and often point and smile, as well.

Members of my staff and our contract speakers have been teaching middle school and high school students about these intelligences. It's part of our public-school programming designed to keep them free from alcohol, other drugs, tobacco, and sex until they marry the person they intend to stay married to forever. These preteens and teens believe more in their ability to make wise choices when they understand how they are smart in numerous ways. Believing in their intelligences motivates them to avoid the negative consequences caused by experimenting with alcohol, other drugs, tobacco, and premarital sex. Understanding these multiple intelligences truly makes a positive impact!

Our prevention programs are also designed to help preteens and teens meet their core, basic needs in healthy ways. This, too, is powerful instruction and directly related to their multiple intelligences.

WHAT ARE OUR CORE NEEDS AND WHY DOES IT MATTER?

God created all of us with five basic needs represented by these questions:

1. Security: *Who can I trust?*
2. Identity: *Who am I?*
3. Belonging: *Who wants me?*

4. Purpose: *Why am I alive?*

5. Competence: *What do I do well?*

Because God designed us with these needs, as I explained in my first book,[1] it's best when we let Him meet them in the order above. Because He is completely trustworthy, we can place our *security* in Him. When we do that, our *identity* is found in Him (e.g., we are saved by faith, forgiven, complete in Christ, unconditionally loved). We *belong* to Him forever, our *purpose* is to glorify Him, and our *competence* is found in who He is, what He does for us, and what He has given us.

These needs must be met. If children don't have healthy ways through which to meet these needs, they'll try to meet them in unhealthy ways. For instance, they may drink and smoke because they think it will help them be accepted by a particular group of peers. They may have sex with a boyfriend or girlfriend because they think it will provide security and meet their belonging need.

Knowing their intelligence strengths allows children to meet their core needs in healthy ways. I'll explain how in chapters three to ten, where one intelligence is the focus of each chapter:

- *Competence:* What do I do well? I describe what strengths are associated with this intelligence and how children can study with it.
- *Identity:* Who am I? I explain what interests, abilities, challenges, and sins are rooted in this intelligence.
- *Purpose:* Why am I alive? I tell how this intelligence affects the way children choose to glorify God. I include how spiritual

disciplines might be practiced and what careers might appeal
to these children.

- *Belonging:* Who wants me? I characterize how this intelligence influences relationships, including how children with
this smart may connect best with God.

- *Security:* Who can I trust? I disclose what things children
with this strength might trust, how you can parent so these
children will trust you, and what can help them trust God
more.

All of us at Celebrate Kids, Inc., enjoy teaching children that
these legitimate needs must be met, and there are healthy and
unhealthy ways to do so. Relying on the eight smarts is a healthy
way to meet these needs. These children begin to discern that
depending on the right people and positive, long-lasting methods is
so much better than looking to the false counterfeits of drugs, alcohol, tobacco, sex before marriage, and other unhealthy behaviors.

A note about the order of the needs mentioned above. This is
the order in which I write about them in each chapter; because,
to explain the eight smarts, I need to begin with what children
with each intelligence do well. That's how you can identify it in
your children. Then you can begin to analyze how the intelligence helps to meet the other four core needs.

However, in reality, our *first* need is for security. This is true
for children as well as adults. Once we know who we can trust,
those people help us figure out who we are. Our identity reveals
the people we may want to relate to, and these belonging relationships often show us how we can fulfill our purpose. Having a
purpose motivates us to develop our competence. We teach these

five basic needs to children in this order. They need to know that they must establish their security first because who they trust influences everything else. I trust all this will make sense as you read chapters three to ten.

WHAT SHOULD
PARENTS DO AND NOT DO?

Before getting to the eight chapters that will detail the smarts in helpful and practical ways, I want to explain one thing you should do and one thing to avoid. These are key processes that relate to all eight smarts.

Crystallizing a Smart

One of your privileges is to work with God to awaken and turn each intelligence into a strength. Dr. Gardner uses the term "crystallize" for this turning.[2] Crystallization can occur more than once for each intelligence. In fact, that's ideal. Something initially crystallizes the intelligence so that part of the mind is alert, but then a few weeks, months, or years later another dynamic person, idea, or experience is used by God to further crystallize the smart. Dr. Gardner calls these the turning points that develop children's talents and abilities. Dr. Armstrong refers to them as the sparks that light intelligences and help to mature them.[3]

You'll often know when an intelligence crystallizes. It will be hard to miss the energy and joy that's released. Your child may keep talking about the same thing (e.g., a planet, new friend, or science experiment) or may want to do the same activity (e.g., finger-paint, reread a new book, or play the piano) for many days in a row.

For example, perhaps your young son saw a worm on the driveway after a rainstorm. He stared at it, touched it, and wanted to know all about it. Perhaps you were concerned about his short attention span until he discovered this worm. Now he is so focused you have a hard time getting him to think about anything else. God used this worm to awaken your son's nature smart. If you spend time with your son exploring worms, go to Web sites for information, and read library books about worms, you crystallize his nature smart further. Think about it this way: The worm on your driveway cracked the nature-smart door open. When you answered your son's questions and got interested with him, the door opened further. If you link his interest in worms to other animals, the door will stay open. This is what I mean by working with God. He gave your son the worm. What did you do with it?

In 2005, violent hurricanes blasted America's Gulf Coast. This followed, by only a few months, the devastating Asian tsunami. As a result, I wonder if we'll see more young people major in meteorology (nature smart) and related fields in the next ten years. Some may major in architecture (picture smart) or engineering (picture smart) with the specific goal of researching how to build buildings and levees to withstand strong, sustained winds and flood waters (logic smart). Some may choose careers in government or community planning (people smart and logic smart) because of what they saw on the news.

I doubt this will occur for children whose parents didn't respond well to their expressed concerns or interests. In contrast, parents who invested in their child's enthusiasm probably crystallized more than one smart. God will often provide experiences for you and your children to respond to. On the other hand, if you recognize your son or daughter hasn't been very interested in one of the intelligences, you'll need to create your own crystallizing experiences.

Paralyzing a Smart

While I do want you to help crystallize your child's smarts, I don't want you to paralyze them. This is a word Dr. Armstrong uses to classify experiences that shut down intelligences.[4] These encounters are often filled with shame, guilt, fear, or anger. Such negative emotions prevent smarts from growing or thriving. Not only do I want you to avoid it, I want you to protect your children from others who may be paralyzers.

Very few parents set out to paralyze their children's intelligences. Yet it happens. Sometimes the smart affected is shut down permanently. It will remain a weak area for the child's lifetime. In other cases, a crystallizing experience can occur that reawakens the intelligence. Isn't it good of God to give us second and third chances?

In general, I think criticism of finished products (e.g., paintings, essays, and projects) and criticism of processes used (e.g., handwriting, the way books and papers are organized, and talking with friends rather than working alone) can paralyze intelligences. (Specific correction is appropriate. Criticism isn't.[5]) Regular punishment of strengths (e.g., movement for body-smart children, talking for word-smart children, and exploring for logic-smart children) can also paralyze the strengths so children no longer use them.

Perfectionism can also shut down smarts because it doesn't

allow children any freedom to explore and grow. Your children know mistakes will most likely occur when they try new things. If they think they need to be perfect, they won't risk trying something new. Do you often respond to your children's attempts by exclaiming, "Just let me do it!"? This decreases their initiative and confidence and suggests they're not good enough. Paralysis sets in. If you notice your children no longer growing in a smart that had once been a strength, see if perfectionism has set in and then talk and teach against it.[6]

Intelligences can also be shut down when children are teased because of their strengths. It doesn't matter who does the teasing. It hurts and plants seeds of doubt. This is also true when out-of-the-box thinking isn't well received. If children often hear, "That would never work" and "We've never done it that way!" they may eventually stop thinking altogether.

Race and gender biases can also paralyze. How unfortunate! For example, two men who have become friends of mine have both detailed for me that their picture-smart strengths weren't affirmed by their parents when they were young. This created great confusion, frustration, and even anger. Joseph is still guarded, not always sure who he can trust with his love of art and design. I'm honored he trusts me, and I hope he'll invite me to go to an art museum with him sometime. I'm not very picture smart, so I've never prioritized doing that, even in some amazing cities of Europe. However, I know Joseph could help me appreciate and understand the art. I would trust him to be patient with me.

Craze was taught that art was irrelevant and frivolous for boys. Because he was always visualizing, daydreaming, and doodling, he believed he wasn't very smart. His mom wanted him to be "the brains," so he was forced into what Craze refers to as his linear (math and accounting) phase. Craze became angry after awhile, as he realized that his mom hadn't been able to recognize an innate gift and tried to instill a different one in him. He had to grieve the loss of time and seek God's understanding. I'm glad he did! When he turned thirty-five, he purchased special pens and paper and started drawing again. I own some of his drawings and they're amazing. Although paralyzed for a long, long time, his picture-smart abilities were still there. Healing and some key conversations and encounters crystallized this smart. Thank God, it's never too late for an intelligence to awaken and be strengthened, focused, and trained!

If you have paralyzed a child's intelligence, the paralysis can be undone if you or others create crystallizing experiences that follow. Although it's ideal when these quickly follow the pain of paralysis, it's never too late, as we can see from Craze's illustration. You must be aware, though, that your child may not quickly respond. This is because the paralyzing experience at least partially destroyed his or her security, identity, belonging, purpose, and competence.

For example, if you've been very negative when interacting with your daughter, she may decide she can't depend on you to meet her need for security. Her identity will no doubt become more negative and she may use "I can't do this . . ." language. She won't be sure she wants to belong to you because of how negative and critical you have been recently. If she had seen herself using the now-paralyzed smart in the future, her sense of purpose will be in doubt. In addition, she'll believe she lacks competence. As you can see, being aware of how core needs are affected is important to reversing the damage. If you paralyze a child's smarts, recognize what you've done (unintentionally or intentionally), apologize and ask to be forgiven, work to reestablish trust, be patient, and do what you can to create a crystallizing experience. You may want to pray, too!

I trust you'll enjoy the next eight chapters and that you'll be deeply encouraged as you discover how you and your children are smart.

I THINK WITH
WORDS...
I AM DEVELOPING MY WORD
SMART!

When I visited Litty and Steve's new home, it was under construction, so we carefully stepped around ladders and over extra lumber. My friends enjoyed pointing out the living and dining rooms, the kitchen, and bedrooms, explaining how the floors, walls, and ceilings would be finished. From several rooms we could see the river and expansive fields behind it. I could easily picture this family and their many guests enjoying this beautiful home and the peaceful location.

My favorite moment occurred when we arrived at the downstairs level. Litty pointed out which spaces would be the guest room, den, and children's bedrooms. When we walked into the girls' room, she pointed out a large closet. Even though it wasn't finished, I could tell it was much larger than most closets in little girls' rooms. Litty looked at me and explained, "This is for Jalisa to play in. She loves playing in her closet and talking as she's playing. She talks all the time! She's excited about all this space!"

Does your daughter talk, even if no one is listening? Does your young son use words you're surprised he already knows? These are evidence that they are most likely word smart, like Jalisa.

Maybe you can relate to my friend, Gabrielle. Her son, Ric, had been talking about his brother. He said, "Red can't do anything and talk at the same time. I can't do something and *not* talk at the same time." I laughed because I can relate! Gabrielle told me that Ric's insight was very accurate. He demonstrates he is word smart with his almost constant chatter.

Gabrielle and her husband, Romane, report that since they have learned and taught their children about multiple intelligences, they're all more patient with each other. They see their differences as just that—differences. Not problems or deficiencies; just ways they were uniquely created by God.

Are you ready to discover how word smart your children are? Remember that within each intelligence there is a hierarchy of smartness. As you read, you can decide if word smart is a strength for your child or if he or she needs help to further awaken and develop it. Perhaps you'll realize that word smart is just not going to be one of your child's strengths. If your child has been exposed to a variety of qualified teachers and helpful experiences and word smart is clearly not a strength, that's okay—if you decide it's okay. If it's not okay, however, your child may feel stupid and unaccepted as you continue to want him or her to achieve what is clearly out of reach. What follows will help you determine where your child is and, more importantly, how to awaken and/or further develop the word-smart part of your child's mind. You'll also learn how this intelligence influences a child's relationship with God.

COMPETENCE:
WHAT DO I DO WELL?

Word-smart children think with words, and when they're excited, they almost always talk. Their excitement may cause them to write, or journal their words, and jot notes to themselves; but talking is the most common way they use their word smart. Although they like talking with others, they don't *need* an audience. They're often content talking to themselves while they play, work, and study. Sometimes you'll hear them, but sometimes they'll admit to talking to themselves inside their heads where no one else can hear.

During my school and church presentations on the eight smarts, I ask children if they are distracted by their own voices—even when they are trying hard to listen to you or their teachers. Many of them laugh and raise their hands. They are amazed that others talk to themselves inside their minds when something excites them.

Teaching is almost always a strength of word-smart children. They may help their sisters and brothers understand something. They may tutor peers or students younger than them. They may also argue, persuade, and entertain with words. Does this sound like one or more of your children?

If your son does not argue well, he still might be quite word smart. As I mentioned in chapter one, none of the intelligences works alone. Each works in tandem with others. For example, arguing is rooted in word *and* logic smart. Persuading is rooted in word *and* people smart. So if your son doesn't argue, it's possible that logic smart is not one of his strengths. However, word smart still could be. It's also possible that his Christlikeness prevents him from arguing, as it should for all of us. We must remember to look for patterns of behavior rather than isolated skills and interests.

Children who are word smart may begin talking at an early age. They may have been curious about writing and learned their letters easily. When older, they write willingly and well and read in their spare time for information and/or enjoyment. They handle most textbooks and assignments successfully, often being able to remember details. They have a large vocabulary, and they speak confidently and listen accurately. They tend to be well informed and often want to share their opinions and ideas with others. Perhaps your children know more than one language. Learning a language easily, retaining the words, and effectively using what they know is further evidence of being word smart. It's all about communication. Their power is language.

Learning and Teaching Methods

When studying and learning with this smart, your child can read, write, and speak about a topic. Word-smart children enjoy listening to others talk about it, recopying or typing lecture notes, and reading other books about the topic, even if the books weren't assigned.

Various teaching methods will be effective with word-smart children, including storytelling, lectures, discussions, putting words on the board during lectures, note-taking strategies, word games, choral reading, reading aloud with great expression, echo reciting, journal writing, drawing upon a variety of books and literary genre, using books on tape, and writing research reports and other kinds of assignments. Debate works, too, which is a positive use of the same skills that often make arguing easy for these children.

Any of the methods listed above will also further awaken and strengthen your child's word-smart strengths. You may need to explain the advantages of the methods so they know why to use one method over another. It will also take longer for a non-word-smart child to use the methods independently and efficiently.

When seeking to strengthen this smart in a child who is less word smart, it's especially important to choose from among many different writing materials. For example, the very children who said they couldn't write their spelling sentences might write detailed and accurate ones when they get to choose gel pens and colored paper. (As you'll come to understand when reading chapter five, this will be especially true if they have picture-smart abilities.)

Make it a priority to read to children and engage them in meaningful conversations, because these activities increase children's listening vocabulary (that is, the words children understand when they hear them even if they can't read or spell them). Because listening vocabulary is one of the best predictors of school success, it's crucial to develop this skill in every child.

IDENTITY: WHO AM I?

Imagine asking a word-smart child to describe him or herself. You're likely to hear responses like these:

- "I talk a lot."   • "I love to write."   • "I enjoy reading."
- "My friends like to talk with me."
- "I like the power of words and the way they feel in my mouth."

(That last one might surprise you, but lots of us who are very word smart will say this. I sometimes ask children, "Are there any words you like to say or feel in your mouth?" Word-smart children are the ones who will say yes.)

It's not surprising that my Grandma Meier gave me the nickname "Chatty Kathy" when I was about two and a half years old. I was quite a talker! Now I earn a living talking and writing. A child's intelligence strengths can often be detected early and be predictive of the future. I enjoyed acting in children's theater when I was a child. I was interested in words and discovered a thesaurus when I was young. I won a reading contest at the public library when I was an elementary school student and was part of the speech team in high school. My Grandpa Meier served as mayor of my city when I was growing up, and I observed him use words only to help people. His example remains a strong motivation for me today.

Can you imagine what might have happened if my parents and teachers had seen my word-smart abilities as irritating problems rather than as strengths to be developed, focused, and trained? What might have happened if I had been raised hearing, "Be quiet . . . shut up . . . go find something to do . . . I'm sick of your talking!"? Would I be speaking and teaching for a living and writing my second book? No. My strengths might have been paralyzed or I might have used them only in unhealthy ways.

Was I sometimes asked to be quiet? Absolutely! Did I sometimes need to leave my brother, parents, and friends alone? Absolutely! Did I sometimes need to listen to my brother? Yes! I'm thankful that he and I were raised to respect others and to develop and use our self-control.

As you can see, word-smart strengths can create challenges for word-smart children and their parents. Not being able to talk to themselves or to engage in conversations can be stressful and distracting for word-smart children. Yet when they talk too much, it may stress others.

Paralysis can also set in due to weaknesses. For example, a student who reads orally in a choppy and slow manner may get teased by classmates. This may cause him or her to avoid reading aloud again. Discouragement may set in for children who struggle to write well creatively and don't have their work displayed on bulletin boards like most of their classmates. Constant vocabulary quizzes can overwhelm and bore children who don't have natural word-smart strengths.

Each of these potentially paralyzing experiences can be undone. Of course, you'll have to observe carefully to recognize the depth of your child's concern so you can strategically enter into the situation. When you read fun material together orally, the pain of classmates' laughter can lift. When you ask the teacher how to help your child improve his or her writing, work together in a casual and nonthreatening way, and celebrate your child's improvements, you can re-ignite your child's enjoyment of writing. You can naturally use and discuss new words, play word games like Scrabble, or complete crossword puzzles together to reawaken your child's willingness to learn new words.

When very young children show strengths with letters, words, talking, and writing, parents tend to feel justifiably excited. As a result, they may focus so much on the development of word-smart skills that they ignore music, picture, body, and nature smarts. Therefore, these children may have just three or four intelligences strongly developed when other children might have five or six on which they can rely.

A child who demonstrates most of the behaviors I included here and in the Competence section could be classified as having word-smart strengths. In contrast, a child who talks a lot, but doesn't necessarily talk to teach or persuade, or who doesn't do well on school assignments, may be an auditory learner instead of a word-smart child. This means she remembers best the things she hears herself say. It's an important strength, but it's not the same as being word smart. While reading these chapters, you'll want to determine whether your children have high or low interest and high or low abilities according to how I explain each smart. Look for *what* they do and *how much* of it they do. Look for *patterns* of ability and interest, not isolated occurrences.

Struggles

As I wrote in chapter one, negatives can point to strengths that are being used badly, in unhealthy ways. For example, word-smart children need to be careful of such sins of the tongue as gossiping, teasing, lying, and arguing. They need to be careful of always needing to have the last word or of talking when they should be listening.

Word-smart children may also tend to be prideful in their intellectual abilities. Feeling good about one's strengths is one thing, but feeling superior to others because of one's gifts is another. Word-smart children may want to show off their knowledge and/or vocabulary. They may be tempted to look down on others who don't appear to have strong literacy skills. They may become unteachable, believing that they know enough because they tend to be well-read.

Do you know children who often struggle with word-smart-related sins? You'll need to find ways to help them stop using their strengths in unhealthy ways. Do look for ways to do it without paralyzing, or shutting down, this intelligence. I'm grateful that didn't happen to me. If it had, I doubt Celebrate Kids, Inc., would have been founded or I'd be writing this book.

My parents looked for opportunities to help me develop my talents and interests. Even my brother and cousin got involved. My grandfather was mayor of the city we lived in during some of my elementary and junior high years. To report on him and other news, my brother and cousin published their own little newspaper called the "Cousins Gazette." I still have vivid memories of being one of their reporters on election nights. With my notepad and pencil, I circulated among the women on the first floor and the men in the basement of my grandparents' home, asking them the questions Dave and Terry assigned to me. As best I could, I wrote down their answers and composed an article, often with Dave's or Terry's help. I remember being thrilled at seeing my name in print when my articles were published. Remember, sometimes emphasizing positive uses of abilities is more effective than talking about the negative ones.

PURPOSE: WHY AM I ALIVE?

Showcasing God

I believe we are alive to glorify God—to showcase who God is—through who we are and through what we do. Children relying on their word-smart gifts will glorify and serve God primarily through learning, speaking, listening, reading, writing, and teaching. For example, they might serve on their school yearbook committee, volunteer to tutor children at a homeless shelter, assist in children's church when they're too old to attend themselves, willingly answer their parents' questions about school, listen attentively to their great-aunt's stories, learn more about biblical concepts, and/ or hone their speaking abilities as part of a speech team. In this last case, they'll especially glorify God when their content is biblical and when they write speeches using their Christian worldview, as this may influence other people's views. They may also learn a second language and serve God during a summer mission trip with people who use that language. Depending on what spiritual gifts and other smarts they have, word-smart children may also please God through their love for His Word, studying the Bible, memorizing Scripture, evangelism, and prayer.

After trusting Christ, one of the primary ways we glorify God is to grow in our relationship with Him. How then might we approach spiritual disciplines for word-smart children? Realizing that other smarts will influence this, as will their spiritual gifts and passions, it's still safe to predict that reading and studying Scripture are probably the easiest disciplines for word-smart children to consistently practice. They'll be most motivated when they have someone to talk with about what they gained from their study and reflection. They may also be very interested in what you're learning, so take advantage of this!

Careers

How young were your children when they first told you what they wanted to be when they grew up? I bet they weren't very old. My young friends, Melody and Grace, have already talked about being ballerinas, zookeepers, and mommies. High schoolers, of course, need to get more focused when thinking about their post-high-school experiences. The question is, what careers will best fit their interests, abilities, gifts, and smarts?

Careers are most fulfilling when there's a good match between the job skills and a person's smarts. Therefore, word-smart children may want to consider careers that involve speaking, listening, reading, and writing. Depending on their other smarts, debating and persuading can also be added to the mix. So, for example, careers with a good fit would include teacher, pastor, counselor, journalist, editor, lawyer, radio or television newsperson, librarian, and politician.[1]

BELONGING: WHO WANTS ME?

Many factors influence whom children choose as friends, including their intelligence strengths. This is partly because their smarts influence what children do in their spare time and what they want to talk about.

Word-smart teens will often prioritize the sharing of knowledge in relationships. As a result, others will probably appreciate them for their knowledge and the meaningful conversations friends can have with them. They're interested in both explaining what they know and learning from others. Therefore, most word-smart teens will want at least two categories of friends: those they can influence and those who can influence them.

Word-smart strengths may contribute to relationship challenges. These children may talk too much and negatively judge those who don't communicate clearly and deeply. Word-smart children can tend to look down on others, especially those who they think don't know as much as they do. In addition, small talk may be very challenging for them because they'd rather be purposeful.

Connecting with God

Word-smart children may connect best with God through His voice and His Word (e.g., Job 37:1–5; Psalm 29; John 15:7). Therefore, reading the Bible to children will be a key. They will benefit from having their own Bible, Bible storybooks, Christian classics such as the Narnia tales by C. S. Lewis, and devotional books. (They may not ask for them, but they will benefit from having them.) Just like their younger brothers and sisters, pre-teens and teens may enjoy having Bible stories and engaging Christian literature read to them. (They may not admit they want you to read to them, but many of them will secretly like it.) Remember that being read to is one of the best ways to increase children's listening vocabulary, so it's very important. Studying Scripture and reading Christian books on their own will also be important to word-smart children.

Because of their learning and listening strengths, word-smart children will often connect with God by attending Sunday school, children's church, midweek church programs, retreats, youth seminars, and vacation Bible school. They'll enjoy learning specific details about God, Jesus Christ, the Holy Spirit, and Bible heroes. They'll want to learn new vocabulary and new ideas and talk about what they learn. Conversations with parents and other adults they respect can help cement the truth and clarify confusing things.

SECURITY: WHO CAN I TRUST?

Trusting Things

All children need to feel secure and to be secure. Without security, concentrating, learning, and life are very challenging. Although children should find their security in God, trustworthy people, and (to some extent) themselves, they may place at least a part of their security in their strengths. For word-smart children, these abilities may include reading and writing, debating, winning people to their side, memorizing trivia, and getting good grades.

Trusting Parents

You need to do what you can to be influential and strong sources of security for your children. For word-smart children, this includes listening closely to their stories and explanations about any number of things. Ask questions to indicate your interest in things your children are passionate about. Being available when they need to think aloud about something will increase their trust in you. Provide them with appropriate, accurate books and other materials related to topics they're interested in, to show them that you're listening and that you care about them.

Depending on your children's ages, you might try writing back and forth when you're concerned about something. This can be a safe and effective way to help older word-smart children and teens open up. You'll be able to share key truths and ask thought-provoking questions. Your children will have time and privacy in which to respond. They may be more willing to answer your questions and to include important information that would be hard for them to say face-to-face. This kind of writing can increase your children's motivation, behavior, and success while increasing their security in you.

Regarding discipline, your children will need you to listen to them and talk with them. Because of their word strengths, you should use descriptive adjectives when including details of their positive and negative behavior. You might want your children to repeat aloud what you tell them, such as the steps to complete their project and the place you need them to put their toys.

Trusting in God

How can we help children who haven't yet trusted Christ for their salvation? And how can we help believing children continue to grow in their faith? What might work best for word-smart children?

Because vocabulary tends to be one of their strengths, teaching them more about God by using His different names might be effective (e.g., Genesis 43:14; Matthew 1:23). They may also be interested to learn that the Bible was first written in Hebrew, Aramaic, and Greek. You could learn some of these words together (e.g., "shalom" is Hebrew for "peace"; "Jehovah" is Hebrew for "God"; "Adonai" is Greek for "the Lord"). Using more than one translation of the Bible, cross-referencing, and the use of a concordance for word studies are other strategies that may increase their confidence in God and His Word.

Family devotions are important for all children, no matter their intelligence strengths. Children who are very word smart may enjoy them more and benefit from them more than others. It will be especially helpful if you involve them in the devotions rather than doing devotions for them. Encourage them to read the Scripture and lesson aloud for everyone. They can also answer some questions and share relevant illustrations.

ABILITY AND INTEREST?

To determine whether children have word-smart strengths, consider both their abilities with and interest in reading, writing, speaking, and listening. Using the grid below, place each family members' name in the most accurate quadrant. Think through what you just read and reflect on what you've consistently observed.

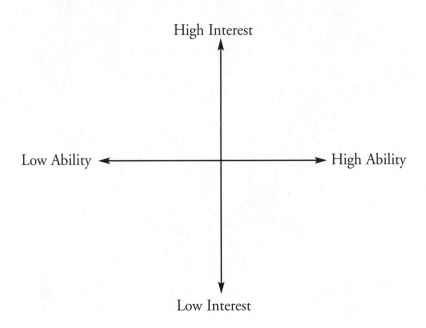

4

I THINK WITH
QUESTIONS...
I AM DEVELOPING MY LOGIC
SMART!

An incident at a workshop illustrates how logic-smart people sometimes respond to other people. As an icebreaker, I asked adults to name a place that was important to them. Several mentioned where they went to college, which generated good-natured teasing from those who graduated from cross-state rivals. Some named their hometown and tried to convince us that it was better than anyone else's. A few chose the city or place where they got engaged. That was fun because we learned that some men were much more romantic than we would have guessed.

My favorite answer came from Marina, a freshman in college who was sitting next to her parents. Her answer, "The kitchen table," caused every head to snap in her direction. I think there were some in the group who probably wondered if Marina had heard my assignment correctly. Some might have thought her answer was ridiculous. After all, she had been to several countries on mission trips. In comparison, how could the kitchen table be an important place?

Those with logic-smart strengths were probably the ones who thought Marina heard my question wrong and who judged her answer as being "ridiculous." Logic-smart people want everything to make sense. Her answer didn't—*to them.*

Logic-smart people often don't realize their strength—or that other people may not be quite so logical as they. Are you so logic smart that you give your children a look of disgust when their thoughts and behaviors don't make obvious sense? When things they do or say seem inappropriate, do you ask, "What?" with a tone that suggests you're amazed at their "stupidity"? This does them no good and can shut down their intelligences. Also, they may stop confiding in you and seeking your opinions.

Logic-smart adults can foster better relationships by learning to say things like, "Keep talking. I need to know more." Or, with a tone of curiosity rather than judgment, "Why did you do that?" Can you learn to temporarily shut off your logic-smartness and listen to understand rather than to judge?

I asked Marina to explain her choice of "the kitchen table." Her parents were especially stunned as she elaborated. Marina explained that she credited her success and happiness to what she learned during conversations with her parents and siblings that took place at the kitchen table.

Now her choice made sense. The logic-smart people were satisfied. So were the others. Actually, I remember us being speechless and humbled. We had judged her too quickly. She answered my question well. It made total sense.

There's much to understand about the logic-smart intelligence, so let's dig in. No matter the age of your children, you will have observed at least some of what I include here. Remember that if you don't think logic smart is a strength for them yet, your strategic involvement can strengthen it. Much of school success relies on logic-smart skills so it's important to cultivate as much of this intelligence as possible. It also has huge implications for a child's spiritual growth, as you'll see.

COMPETENCE:
WHAT DO I DO WELL?

Logic-smart children probably showed commonsense reasoning at a young age. Their strengths are rooted in thinking, and today they might admit to thinking just for fun! They're usually not afraid of exploring unknown topics. They will often dive right in and explore new ideas. They can brainstorm questions easily, even helping parents think through vacation plans or other major decisions.

Logic-smart children think with questions and when they're excited, they ask more questions. Because answering written questions and discussion questions plays a significant role in school, many logic-smart children earn excellent grades.

These children have a high need to know. As a result, they're often stressed when they don't know what they think they should. For example, not having details for an assignment that's due soon is frustrating. So is not understanding content from one of their classes. They can also be concerned about and distracted by what's going on at home. If you seem to be fighting, a grandmother is calling more often than normal, or a sibling is angry all the time, logic-smart children can be unnerved.

Because these children *need* things to make sense, they may often ask "Why?" You may interpret these "Why?" questions as defiance, and they sometimes can be. Often the questions spring from children's logic-smartness. These children genuinely want to know why you don't want them to run in the backyard, why they're going to visit their cousins, or why you're serving spaghetti for dinner. Paralysis can certainly set in if you regularly answer their "Why?" questions with statements such as, "Don't bother me now" and "I'll tell you if you need to know." I've had many conversations with parents concerned because their children don't seem to be thinking on their own. As we talk, they realize their responses have discouraged independent, creative, and critical thinking. Apologizing and choosing to *really* hear and answer their children's questions can reverse the trend.

My great-aunt Ola wanted things to make sense. She struggled when they didn't. Even though it was probably thirty-five years ago, I have vivid memories of talking with her about television commercials. She loved finding things that didn't make sense in them. I can still remember her pointing out an ad for a brand of baking soda. She laughed and laughed—something she didn't do often. The spokesperson was encouraging people to pour it down the drain to freshen it, so she said, "Pour the box down the drain." Aunt Ola loved telling me how that made no sense. "You can't pour the *box* down the drain! Who wrote that?!"

Logic-smart children need something worth thinking about. If they're not kept challenged and engaged, they'll find something on their own to think about and analyze. For example, they may try taking apart color markers to determine why and how they work on only one type of paper. Do you understand why I often say bored logic-smart children can be dangerous?

If you or your child's science teacher says, "Don't put those things in the bowl yet," logic-smart children often respond, either verbally or in their mind, "Why not? What might happen?!" Then before anyone realizes it, they put everything in the bowl to see what happens! And something happens! Adults' responses to these occurrences will either paralyze the logic-smart part of the mind or expand and develop it further. Can you picture and even hear in your mind a response that shuts down a child's logic-smart thinking and one that would strengthen it?

As is demonstrated by that "why not?" illustration, many logic-smart children enjoy science and are able to easily think scientifically. Their strengths lie in their accurate, research-driven, and cause-effect thinking. Their strengths also lie in experimenting. They enjoy analyzing, predicting, and inventing.

For some of the same reasons, math is a strength of logic-smart children. (Teaching young children their numbers and encouraging them to count aloud are examples of how to awaken logic smart.) These math strengths might have been obvious early, when numbers, adding, telling time, and understanding money didn't frustrate your son. As he gets older, you might see that estimating and statistics (e.g., professional baseball stats) are strengths. Calculations may come easily. These children greatly appreciate the logical nature of math. For instance, $2+2 = 4$, $22+22 = 44$, and $222+222 = 444$. Always. This is the child you want with you when you're out to dinner with friends. Without a calculator, he can accurately determine what each person owes for dinner and the tip.

Success with some types of math depends on other intelligences. For example, word-smart skills are necessary for story problems and picture-smart strengths help children learn shapes and geometry. It's for these reasons that I encourage children to not believe or say things like, "I'm not good at math." Plus, because of other learning styles or attention issues, memorizing math facts might not be easy. That doesn't mean these children aren't logic smart. They may just need to grow into it. Next semester or next week, math might be easier because of their smarts and the type of math assigned.

Within reading and writing, logic-smart children's interests typically lie more with nonfiction than fiction. Because they are natural problem solvers, mysteries might be their favorite fiction. They also might prefer these types of television shows.

Learning and Teaching Methods

To study and learn best with their logic-smartness, children should ask and answer questions. Their motivation will increase when they look for problems to solve. Most logic-smart children will benefit from "What if?" thinking. Statements that begin with "I wonder . . ." can also stimulate their curiosity and engage their minds. At a younger age than other children, these children naturally make comparisons and contrasts, analyze information, sequence ideas, and discover cause-effect relationships. "If/then" thinking is one of their strengths.

The careful use of thinking verbs can be especially motivational and productive for logic-smart children. In other words, rather than telling them to "just think" about their reading assignment, it's wise to tell them how to *specifically* think. For instance, they can define, distinguish, evaluate, and predict. One of the most efficient ways to increase children's logic-smartness might be to teach them how and why to think, as you use these and other verbs. Add these words to vocabulary lists and teach and test them like other words.

To engage the logic-smart part of the mind, children benefit from brain teasers, experiments across the curriculum, time lines, research, data collections, debate, and numbers in more than math classes. You can ask questions so children discover logical connections between ideas and between subjects being studied. So can teachers. Posing problems to be solved tends to work well. Because reasoning is their power, it's important to ask children why and how they came up with their solutions.

If their reading skills aren't strong, logic-smart children can become frustrated because they're genuinely interested in truth, and they typically want to do well in school. Sometimes reading books about the same topic, but written at an easier level, will help them handle their reading assignments more successfully. These easier materials will make their grade-level texts manageable by introducing needed vocabulary words and background knowledge. For example, college students can read high-school-level texts, and middle school and high school students can find the same topics covered in textbooks for younger students or in library books. Web sites and DVDs can help, too.

Methods that are easy and appealing to logic-smart children are the same ones that can awaken and strengthen this intelligence for other children. Apply the methods carefully, though.

For example, if you ask "What if?" questions with children who are and aren't logic smart, logic-smart children may so quickly provide answers and ideas that the other children won't benefit from this technique. By the end, they might be less confident than when the lesson began. Of course, teachers can strategically call on the less logic-smart children at the right times, carefully assign children to small groups, and teach them how to succeed with these methods. That's a key. We shouldn't assume children will be successful. We need to teach them how to succeed.

Answering children's questions enhances their logic smart. As often as you can, take advantage of children's expressed curiosity, even when their questions appear to be off-task. Also, help them think about and research answers to their own questions. This can further grow their curiosity, knowledge, and logic-smart thinking skills.

The asking of questions is an essential life skill. If children tend to *not* ask questions, introducing them to fun trivia and fascinating facts can encourage them to do so. Too many children tell me they stop asking questions because parents and teachers respond too often with statements like these: "You don't need to know that." "Look it up yourself." "That's not important."

Children tell me that "That's not important!" is one of the most hurtful things parents and teachers have said to them. When we talk about it, children comment, "The question was important to me or I wouldn't have asked it." Not allowing children to ask questions and not taking their questions seriously are easy ways we shut down the logic-smart intelligence. It can be reawakened with an apology and some fun, interactive question-and-answer times. Be patient. Your children will have to learn that you will begin taking their questions seriously.

Many children tell me they're usually being truthful when they courageously admit they don't understand something. They resent it when you or teachers accuse them of simply being lazy or of not thinking. Do you realize how intimidating and discouraging it can be for your non-logic-smart daughter, who bravely admits she is confused, to have you proclaim, "If you would just think about it!"? If she has been thinking as best she knows how, your words will wound her and deeply discourage her. Now she might not risk admitting she needs help again. Therefore, she will not grow as much as she could have.

Providing objects and ideas to explore and think about can further awaken and expand the logic-smart part of children's minds. Open-ended exploration, where many conclusions can result, will be an especially good starting place. Field trips, so they can observe and interact with knowledge firsthand, also enhance this intelligence.

Logical and organized parents and teachers are important to logic-smart children, because these children can get easily frustrated and angry when things don't make sense. Children without logic-smart strengths will also benefit from interacting with logic-smart adults. This role modeling is important.

IDENTITY: WHO AM I?

Children with logic-smart strengths may answer the "Who am I?" identity question by telling you about their explorations and the many things they wonder about. You might hear about their excellent grades. They might admit to irritating friends or teachers with their constant questions. They might share their frustrations about policies or happenings at home, school, church, and in life that they think are unfair.

Logic-smart children may admit they don't like to read or that reading is hard for them. This is not always the case, but it sometimes is. Because they like it when things make sense, they may get frustrated by stories that make no sense to them (e.g., stories with talking animals). If the elementary school reading program uses mostly fiction, this can turn logic-smart children off to reading. Many logic-smart children will do better with nonfiction than fiction (e.g., a book with facts about cars rather than a story about cars). Therefore, if your logic-smart son or daughter is struggling to learn to read, try using nonfiction. (Most young children will do very well with make-believe stories. Watch for a possible shift as your child ages.)

My sister-in-law, Debbie, reads about as much as I do. She often reads fiction. She often recommended fiction books to me, and I'm sure she was frustrated when I wasn't interested. Then she heard me teach about multiple intelligences. Now she understands that I don't enjoy fiction because I'm very logic smart and I'm not very picture smart. Wanting (or even needing) everything to make logical sense and not being able to see the action come alive makes most fiction less than appealing to me. I read almost constantly. What do I read? Nonfiction journal articles and books related to my work. It rarely feels like work, though. I enjoy this kind of reading as much as Debbie enjoys reading fiction.

Because logic-smart children can struggle when things don't make sense and when "rules" don't work, spelling and phonics can challenge them. Unless logic-smart children are also picture smart and they can remember what the words look like, they may struggle. This can be true even if they are word smart.

For example, even though many children are still being taught that the first vowel makes the long sound when two vowels are together, the letters "ea" can make numerous sounds: steak, meal, dead, early, react. Even with the same exact letters in a word, the sound "ea" changes: "read" and "read." And "red" is also pronounced like "read." No wonder some children struggle to learn how to read! And then there are words like "there," "their," and "they're." These, too, can discourage logic-smart children.

Spelling is a weakness with which I'm familiar. Word smart and logic smart are both strengths of mine. Because I'm not as picture smart, spelling isn't easy for me. I definitely rely on the spell-check feature in my computer, my fabulous dictionary and thesaurus software, staff members who proof some of my work before I send it out, and editors. Why do I use a thesaurus if my problem is spelling? Because that's how I sometimes find words I want to use that I can't spell. I look up "famous" to find "acclaimed" (one "c" or two?) and "renowned." (Is it spelled with a "u" or a "w"?)

Even though spelling is not a natural strength for me, I'm a writer. I tell children all the time that they must not let their weaknesses win. They must lead with their strengths and they must be obedient. Because God has called me to write, I write. No excuses! I work to remember words I use often and humble myself by relying on others. Children can do this, too.

Struggles

One of the greatest strengths of logic-smart children, their problem-solving abilities, can easily ensnare them if they're not careful. Remember what I explained in chapter one? In my programs about this topic for children, I often include that much of the evil done in the world is done by logic-smart people who are really stupid. They laugh. Then it sinks in. Logic-smart children must be very careful. It's easier than we think to cross over the line from good to evil. Not only can logic-smart children solve problems, they can create them—often without being caught.

Another strength, curiosity, can lead to sin when children aren't guarded. Self-control is essential. Being curious about how things work can actually contribute to their decision to smoke, try illegal drugs, and/or experiment with sex before marriage. At a simpler level, curiosity can cause them to listen to conversations not meant for them and look at things they shouldn't.

Pride can set in, specifically, intellectual pride (believing they have all the answers) and spiritual pride (believing they have figured out God). Judging others, arguing to make their points and/or to defend themselves, and being angry when they're confused are other sin temptations.

Logic-smart children may also tend to worry because thinking and analyzing come easily to them, and they like it when things make sense. I can relate to this! I've joked with friends and coworkers, telling them, "I'm analyzing." But it's not funny. Sin is sin. I might call it analyzing, but sometimes it's worrying.

Logic-smart children can also get into trouble by challenging and testing adults. Children laugh with me when I ask them what they might think if a parent ordered, "Don't step over that line!" I demonstrate by putting one foot over an imaginary line and saying: "I'm not all the way over the line. I'm straddling it. I know. I looked the word up in a dictionary. It won't be right if my dad gets mad. And if I step *on* the line, I'm also not over the line. If I do that and get yelled at, I'll just tell my dad he's wrong." The amount of laughter indicates that many children think like that! I then make the important point that they have a responsibility to do what's right. Intelligence strengths are no excuse for sin. Obedience is right!

PURPOSE: WHY AM I ALIVE?

Showcasing God

Logic-smart children can glorify and serve God in many ways that involve asking and answering questions to discover, explain, and apply truth. They might engage in helpful research, not just for school papers, but to help friends who may struggle with eating disorders or grief over the death of a grandparent.

These children might design systems and procedures for a school club or keep statistics for their school's volleyball or basketball teams. Their ability to reason things through will help them be effective team leaders, perhaps for a church youth group. (Remember that intelligences don't work alone. Logic-smart children will be more effective leaders when they also have people-smart strengths.)

As mentioned, logic-smart children can tend to quickly judge irresponsible and illogical people as foolish and even stupid. Therefore, logic-smart children glorify God when they are patient with those who don't have the same strengths they have, when they don't laugh at what they think are foolish conclusions, and when they advise rather than laugh at those who get wrong answers.

God is also glorified when logic-smart children choose to believe in Him even when they don't know everything they want to know. This is perhaps the best way they glorify God—to obediently choose to trust the leading of the Holy Spirit and trust Christ alone for their salvation even when questions remain. This is my testimony. I often say it this way: I turned off my head and turned on my heart and chose, out of obedience, to simply believe, despite the fact that not all my questions were answered. Then I turned my head back on! I'm grateful that the Holy Spirit teaches us and that we can learn more after we believe (e.g., Proverbs 2:1–6; Proverbs 9:10; and John 14:26). Logic-smart children should be told that they don't need to know everything about God in order to believe Him or to believe in Him.

God is glorified when logic-smart children grow to become more like His Son, Jesus Christ. Bible study and meditating on Scripture will probably be key ways these children will mature. Another will be by listening well to sermons and messages and studying the topics on their own. They will probably prefer nonfiction books to "cute devotionals." They might dig deeply into one subject, reading several books on prayer, for example, and/or they may choose to read and study everything by one author they like.

Careers

Logic-smart children may be most fulfilled in careers that involve the mind. Because of their ability to formulate and ask questions and then critique answers, counseling, teaching, researching, and careers involving public safety such as police work and forensic science may appeal to them. If they are also body smart, then careers like auto mechanic, plumber, and phone-repair technician make sense. Careers involving science and math also come to mind. Other intelligence strengths, passions, and spiritual gifts can influence which of these will be the best fit: pharmacist, electrician, accountant, bookkeeper, appraiser, computer programmer, banker, engineer, auditor, and meteorologist.

BELONGING: WHO WANTS ME?

Since solving problems is a definite strength of logic-smart children, and it's often part of their reputation, this may be the basis for their relationships. Because they provide accurate and helpful information and commonsense advice, those with significant needs or with immature problem-solving skills may choose them as friends. They're usually excellent brainstormers and can help others think of new questions that enhance their understandings and projects.

The logic-smart questioning and problem-solving strengths can easily become a stumbling block when taken to the extreme. For example, logic-smart children may only want to relate to those who have problems because they feel important and better about themselves when they help them. This, of course, isn't healthy.

Humor and small talk can be challenging for logic-smart children. Some of them may judge humor and some forms of fun as unnecessary or frivolous. They often think things are stupid that other children find funny. This can be stressful because they don't laugh when others do, and they can feel like they don't fit in. Small talk can bore them, since they want to talk about things worth thinking about.

Although it may be more common with logic-smart adults than children, these children also need to be careful of analyzing people rather than loving them. A number of years ago, a friend of mine sent me a letter to explain that our friendship was at risk. I was surprised, but as I read her letter, she made total sense. We became friends during a time in her life when she benefited from my problem-solving skills. She talked about what was going on, and I asked questions and provided solutions. It became a natural rhythm for our conversations. However, in her letter, she explained that she was feeling like a problem I was trying to solve or a project I was trying to finish. She asked me to listen and love her instead.

I remain grateful to this day that my friend trusted me with her pain, believed I could change, and didn't just end our friendship. After many weeks of honest conversations and some important decisions, a new rhythm was established and we are closer today than we were then. (For a long time, I prayed before calling her, asking God to enhance my listening skills and compassion while temporarily quieting my questioning and problem-solving skills. I chose to provide sympathy and compassion rather than solutions.)

I often talk about this issue during high school assemblies. Many children tell me their parents interact with them as I did with my friend. They admit to being glad their parents have problem-solving and thinking strengths, but there are times when they'd just like to be heard. Some admit they stop sharing with their parents to avoid the inevitable interrogation and problem-solving session. Is this relevant in your family dynamic?

Connecting with God

Connections to God for logic-smart children will be very similar to those for word-smart children. They'll most likely appreciate God for His truth and wisdom (e.g., John 14:6; Romans 11:33; Colossians 2:2–3). In fact, they must be careful of the tendency to be satisfied with merely knowing *about* God. They must move on to knowing God, believing in God, and loving God. They may struggle with principles like grace, mercy, and unconditional love. Studying these and having them explained and modeled can help children understand and believe in these heart principles. Logic is not enough for a complete connection with God; they also need the heart's feelings and responses.

SECURITY: WHO CAN I TRUST?

Trusting Things

Because logic-smart children can almost always find something that isn't trustworthy and logical in people, I think it's quite easy for them to trust in their strengths instead of in people. For example, they might meet their need for security in their problem-solving abilities, math and/or science understandings, and grades. Winning arguments and being able to defend themselves with well-thought-through reasons may make the list, too.

Trusting Parents

Parents who take time to answer their children's questions are more likely to gain their children's trust than those who don't. Dismissing children's questions and not allowing them to explore safe things they want to think about are quick ways to shut down, or paralyze, this intelligence. In contrast, researching with them what they're curious about and providing relevant and accurate information will positively affect these children. Helping them learn to handle confusion, seeming contradictions, and other things that violate their need for logic will also be wise. It's vital that you model calm in the midst of your storm, admit the questions you have during difficult times, and teach them how you cope when things don't appear to make sense.

Some ways to avoid and perhaps even solve discipline and motivation problems include asking empowering questions, posing problems to solve, using cause-effect thinking, explaining your rationale, and asking for their children's reasoning.

Trusting in God

For logic-smart children to trust Christ for their salvation, their parents, pastors, Sunday school teachers, and small-group leaders must be open to hearing any and all questions the children have about God, spiritual issues, and themselves. Children must have their questions honored. Parents can research answers with them by using Bible study tools and talking with pastors and Sunday school teachers. Children should also know that you pray, asking God for His wisdom. In the midst of these conversations, parents should point their children to the heart as often as possible. Remember—head knowledge is more comfortable for logic-smart children, but their hearts must also be engaged.

Logic-smart children may be fascinated and comforted by the logic and consistency between the Old and New Testaments (e.g., prophecies in the Old that have been proven true in the New, the God of Daniel is the same as the God of Revelation). The consistency of the four Gospels and the recurring themes in Paul's writings are also relevant to these children. A study of Job will show them that there's nothing wrong in asking tough questions, but faith is possible even when we don't understand everything. This is, perhaps, the greatest challenge for logic-smart children. Christianity doesn't always make a lot of sense!

ABILITY AND INTEREST?

Using what you've read and what you observe, place your children's names in the most accurate quadrant to indicate their logic-smart abilities and interests. Include your name, too. You might want to immediately think about how to share this evaluation and logic-smart information with your children. Depending on their ages, they may be able to think with you about what might help to increase their interest and/or ability.

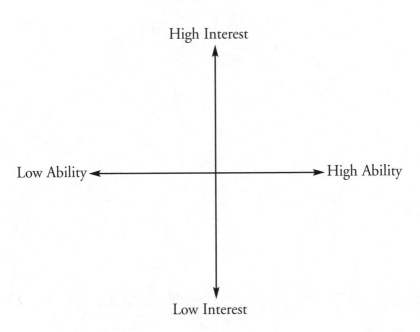

5

I THINK IN
PICTURES...
I AM DEVELOPING MY PICTURE
SMART!

Maddie was among those parents and teachers who attended one of my multiple intelligence seminars some years ago. Years earlier she was one of my college students, and we had stayed in touch. She was now thirty years old and teaching dance to children. Within days after the seminar, I received a long handwritten letter from her. Tears still come when I read it. Her words are a powerful reminder to me of how important it is for parents and teachers to understand multiple intelligences.

Here's part of what Maddie wrote:

> By the time I was a sophomore in high school I was pretty broken. The classes I excelled at, such as creative writing and history, seemed to be few and far between. The required classes like algebra and

chemistry slew me. I can't tell you how many tears I shed. I was, in my own opinion, and seemingly in the opinions of my teachers, not very smart. C grades were common in math and science. As for the occasional A's I did receive, those came out of classes like choir and other subjects that came easily to me. I never imagined that kind of information was easy for me to process because I was smart. I thought the material was easy.

As a junior in the second-rate history course (I wasn't smart enough to be in the first-rate course), I watched one day as my history teacher stood in front of our class and assisted us in deciding which courses to take the following year. He was careful to mention that Western civilization was a very difficult course, and he didn't think that any of us would enjoy it. To prove his point, he cited examples that were supposed to discourage us. "I mean—you have to learn all this stuff like who painted the Mona Lisa and . . ." Before I knew what I was doing, I said "daVinci." Mr. Green looked at me. My classmates looked at me. I, relatively shy, swallowed and let Mr. Green bring it back on track with, "Well, more than that. You have to know stuff like who designed Monticello." I matter-of-factly said, "Thomas Jefferson." Mr. Green looked at me. My classmates looked at me. He continued, "You have to know stuff like who painted the ceiling of the Sistine Chapel." Without missing a beat, I responded, "Michelangelo." None of the answers came out of impertinence. They came out of surprise. Weren't these answers common knowledge?

After all was said and done, I had answered all of the questions well-intending Mr. Green was trying to use to dissuade us. The catch of this little story? After getting those sample questions right, I decided to *not* take the class. Why? Well, everyone said it was really hard and only the smart kids took it. So I didn't. No one came to me and said, "Boy, you're a visual thinker and have the ability to analyze details. This is the class for you!" For the record, I later took a similar class in college and aced it!

Can you relate to anything Maddie shared? Do your children know the answers to Mr. Green's questions, and do they understand they're smart if they do? Do you see how helpful being picture smart can be even though these abilities are downplayed in many schools? Can you feel how discouraging it can be when these strengths are devalued?

COMPETENCE: WHAT DO I DO WELL?

Picture-smart children think with their eyes. They pay attention to visuals in books, such as pictures, diagrams, maps, charts, and illustrations. That's how Maddie knew the answers to Mr. Green's questions. She thinks in pictures, as do other picture-smart people.

Picture-smart children may also use their visual strengths to examine objects and pay close attention during demonstrations. They can learn a lot from these and they'll probably retain the information. However, children also tell me that some objects and demonstrations are so engaging and distracting that they interfere with their ability to pay attention to their teachers' instructions. Self-control will help them stop looking and start listening.

These children may also study irrelevant things with their eyes. For example, if a history teacher's dress has an unusual design, her picture-smart students may analyze it instead of listen to her. Children have told me about spots on shirts, crooked pictures in the kitchen, and dead flowers on tables interfering with their ability to concentrate. They tell me it's not easy for them to turn off their eyes.

Strengths of picture-smart children also include their ability to visualize pictures, diagrams, and colors *in their minds*. For example, if you easily create visuals for the words that follow, it's because you're picture smart: candle, stagecoach, and volcano. Because everyone is picture smart to some extent, everyone can create some kind of visuals for these words. Very picture-smart children will *want* to create them and they'll do it easily, using accurate details and rich colors. Others of us might need to make a concerted effort to merely sketch outlines in our minds, and it will take time for us to do so.

In my "How Am I Smart?" school programs, I ask children who can see a volcano when I just say the word, and about 75 percent of the children raise their hands. I then ask them to describe the color of the lava as it erupts. I'm often impressed with how quickly and confidently many of them can do this. "It's mostly red-orange with some ruby red sections." "Mine is more orange-red and it's almost fluorescent where it's hottest." "Some sections of my lava are so dark, they look black."

Those who are very picture smart don't intend for words and sights to trigger visuals that pop into their minds. It just happens automatically. Visualizing is one of their powers. Often, the visuals help their comprehension, retention, and enjoyment, but this ability can backfire. When the images are irrelevant to the lessons, they don't help. Besides that, they can cause children to daydream.

All children daydream at times. What triggers their daydreams differs by intelligence. So does how they daydream.

Word-smart children describe their daydreams as "conversations with myself." Children with picture-smart talent describe theirs as "beautiful moving pictures" and "movies with action that's more interesting than what my parents or teachers are talking about."

When children get excited, they tell me they add to the pictures in their minds—another color and shape in the design, another dinosaur in the swamp, a blooming flower by the front door, or a musician on stage. They also tell me "the movie in my mind plays faster." They'll often doodle faster, louder, or with more colors or designs when they're excited.

All picture-smart children share this strength of seeing and designing in their minds. Some picture-smart children also draw and create. They're more picture smart than those who can't. Some children are into colors and art, and they may sketch, draw, or paint with accurate and beautiful detail. Others are into flowcharts and diagrams and are more likely to draw intricate designs and build with blocks. Within picture smart, this is my strength. There are some who struggle to do any of this!

When I think about picture-smart strengths, my nephew, Andy, comes to mind. As a small boy, he spent hours playing with his toy trains and redesigning their layouts. He also built complicated structures with blocks of all sorts. He could see them before he created them. I think he had a story to go with each one. If his parents had declared, "Pick all that up!" or "Aren't you going to do anything important today?" paralysis of his picture smart could have set in. He has now matured to certain video games that rely on his picture-smart abilities. These strengths have also helped him in school. He can remember a chemical's structure because he can still see it in his mind after closing his textbook. He can better understand the algebra problem because he can picture the lines intersecting as the teacher describes them. As you can see, it's a good thing that he activated this intelligence when playing as a young boy and that he was allowed to do so.

Andy's picture-smart strengths have also helped him succeed in athletics. He is able to picture the basketball play as his coach describes it. When playing soccer, he can more accurately picture the trajectory of the ball after it's kicked than the athlete who lacks picture-smart abilities. I'm not at all surprised that Andy is thinking about majoring in engineering when he begins college in a few years. Can you see the connections?

As my nephew's example demonstrates, the picture-smart power to observe is valuable in many classes. In math, observation skills might mean that a plus sign is not misread as a minus sign. In art, the picture-smart person will notice size and not just color. In music, picture-smart children won't miss the flat sign in front of the note.

Picture-smart strengths can make letter and number identification easy for young children. That's one reason it definitely pays to activate this part of the brain early in life. For children who struggle to discern between "b and d," "was and saw," and/or "6 and 9," you want to strengthen their picture-smart skills rather than simply drilling them on these letters, words, and numbers. Encouraging them to color and paint and create shapes and designs out of pipe cleaners, popsicle sticks, and the like can help. Talking about designs and shapes you see in the world around you and then tracing them, trying to draw them, and/or building them with blocks will also awaken your children's picture-smart intelligence. Drawing their attention to triangles and pictures like birds that "point" in different directions is also a good idea.

Remember that we always rely on more than one intelligence at a time. For instance, if children with picture-smart strengths are also very body smart, they'll probably have excellent eye-hand coordination. Therefore, they'll have legible handwriting and create sculptures more readily than others could. They may also enjoy taking things apart and putting them back together. They'll be most successful at this when they also use their logic smart.

There's more. A picture-smart, logic-smart combination can make geometry easier. This can show up early, when only some young children easily learn that squares and rectangles are different. Trigonometry, calculus, and advanced algebra are also math disciplines in which children will need to use picture-smart skills. An important implication follows. Children who want to improve their understanding and grades in these courses may be well-advised to develop their picture-smartness rather than just working on math principles.

Children with picture-smart strengths probably enjoy creative writing, fiction, and history. The action comes alive in their mind's eye. I thought it was as if the words on the page drew the pictures. However, a friend who is very picture smart told me, "The words jump off the page and form the pictures." Action also comes alive when they read the Bible to themselves or someone reads it to them. These are the children who have seen the coat of many colors, Jonah in the fish, and Jesus walking on water. Ask your children about this. You might be very encouraged by their vivid descriptions. They might also laugh when they see Jesus turning into a piece of bread as you're teaching how Jesus is "the bread of life" (John 6:35). I'll never forget one child who declared, "And, Dr. Kathy, He is not boring white bread! He is multigrain bread like my mom makes me eat!" (Just as with your responses to the logic-smart experimenter you're raising, responses to comments like these from picture-smart children can either paralyze the intelligence or encourage children to use it more. As I often teach, the words we speak and the words we don't speak change lives. We must be alert and careful!)

Learning and Teaching Methods

To activate the picture-smart part of the brain when learning and studying, encourage activities that involve watching, drawing, sketching, visualizing, and noticing descriptive words and details used by teachers and authors. Focusing on pictures, diagrams, maps, displays, and demonstrations is another way to train this intelligence. Teachers can use these tools, and children can be encouraged to find or create them for themselves and/or to share with classmates.

Telling picture-smart children to "Close your eyes and see" helps them draw upon their natural ability. They can see the word they're trying to learn, the data they're trying to memorize, the order of events for their history test, and the answer on the page. We can also say, "Picture this" at the beginning of our instructions. When doing homework and taking tests, children can learn to ask themselves, "Does it look right?" Teachers and parents can also ask this question to stimulate their picture-smart thinking.

It's appropriate to use art, design, and color throughout the curriculum. For example, as an appropriate in-class activity or homework assignment, children can draw the definition of vocabulary or spelling words. If they're studying different structures and their vocabulary words are *apartment building, condominium, duplex, warehouse,* and *factory,* one night they could sketch each structure. On another, their assignment could be to write definitions of each word. On another, they could be challenged to use all the words in one meaningful story. Children with picture-smart strengths will enjoy the drawing and creative writing tasks and benefit from them. Other children will profit because it engages a part of the mind that is typically not involved in learning vocabulary. This will improve their understanding and memory. It's not necessary to evaluate the quality of the drawing, just the accuracy. In other words, does the apartment building look more like a warehouse? Is the duplex distinguishable from a house? Be careful here. A quick way to paralyze the picture-smart intelligence is to ask, while looking at a picture, "What is that?"

If your daughter forgets "penny" ends with a "y" and not an "e," she can use a yellow crayon to make each "y" when studying the word. This color aid might remind her of the "y" when taking the spelling test. Another idea is to teach younger students to do what many college students do: use highlighters. They might not be able to use them in their books, but they can on their lecture notes, handouts, and study guides. Highlighting main ideas, cause-effect relationships, descriptive adjectives, and any number of other things may help children remember ideas. They can either use their favorite color throughout or color-code by using more than one color (e.g., main ideas in yellow, vocabulary words in green).

Another effective approach is to use thinking verbs that tend to activate and strengthen picture-smart reasoning and reflecting, such as *create, demonstrate, describe, illustrate,* and *show.* When reading their texts and reviewing their notes, children can make up statements or questions their teachers might use on tests. For example, "*Illustrate* the process used to make paper." "*Describe* the story's setting, including details that, if changed, would have changed the story." "How could you *demonstrate* the same level of faith Daniel had?" If you're familiar enough with what your children are studying, you can make up questions and statements like these, too.

Everything already mentioned can also help children who aren't natural picture-smart thinkers. However, with these children it's important to teach the benefits of visualizing and give them time to visualize. I can testify to both of these. I've chosen to develop this intelligence over the past several years. It's not that I never used it; it's just never been terribly important to me. I used pictures and visual thinking when teaching my second-grade students, middle-school athletes, and college students—but I didn't depend on this smart when studying and learning for myself. I've been motivated to strengthen this smart by interacting with picture-smart people and realizing how many children have these strengths.

Choosing to visualize has enhanced my understanding of Scripture and improved my memory work. The word "choosing" is a key. Naturally gifted picture-smart learners don't have to choose to visualize. The visuals will automatically appear in their minds, often whether they want them to or not. However, some of us need to make a conscious choice to think with our eyes. The picture-smart intelligence will never be in my top four or even six, but I have more of it now than I did even six months ago. Motivation and necessity were keys. This chapter would have been virtually impossible to write without some personal understanding! Because God generously equipped us with all eight intelligences, I was able to tap into that part of my mind. You can encourage your children to do the same.

IDENTITY: WHO AM I?

When meeting people for the first time, picture-smart children may tell you about their artistic pursuits and what they've recently drawn, painted, or created. They may talk about their imaginations, creativity, and academic struggles. Because they tend to have a hard time listening for long stretches, they may announce, "I'm bored a lot!" You might also hear about their soccer and drama skills. They often have a keen sense of humor because of the pictures they see in their minds. They might tell you about this.

Because so much time in school is spent thinking and talking about words and numbers, picture-smart children who are not also word smart and logic smart may struggle. Not all words and numbers conjure up visual images, so they can become frustrated. Learning fatigue can also set in. To help, we can use stories and pictures to teach math facts. Three intelligences will be working together, and when children intentionally use more than one intelligence, they will almost always learn more accurately and retain it longer.

Here's an example from a curriculum called "Times Tables the Fun Way," which successfully uses stories and pictures to teach math facts. For the fact 6x6 = 36, they use a clever picture with this story: Two sixes walked across the hot desert to visit their cousin. When they arrived, they were very thirsty sixes. What's 6x6? Thirsty-six! (You can learn more about this program at www.CityCreek.com.)

Sometimes strengths can actually cause learning problems. For example, children who are picture smart may decide that "monkey" is spelled m-o-n-k-e-y because there's a "tail" at the end of the word, just like a monkey has a tail. Then what might happen? They might read "money," "Mikey," and "many" as "monkey," because these words also have "tails." They might learn "elephant" on their vocabulary list only because it's the longest word. They won't know it when it's placed among other long words.

Struggles

Picture-smart children need to guard their eyes. They can sin by looking at what they shouldn't. They might also tend to judge people and things based only on appearance. This "judging a book by its cover" isn't God's way; 1 Samuel 16:7 says God looks at the heart. Another potential trap: Because their visual strengths allow them to see details, they may become critical and negative, eager to point out visual mistakes in someone's wardrobe, decorating, or school project.

PURPOSE: WHY AM I ALIVE?

Showcasing God

When our children see God for who He is, as their Creator who intentionally chose their intelligences for them, they should be more motivated to use their smarts for His purposes. They can praise Him and give Him honor through their choices and by maturing in Christlikeness. He is worthy!

Picture-smart children can glorify, praise, honor, and magnify God by using their eyes to help themselves and others, rather than to hurt. When they create art that honors God and motivates others to think about Him, He is well pleased.

Picture-smart children might develop their skills so they can serve as photographers for their school's Web site, designers for their school yearbook, and wardrobe and stage assistants for their school's spring musical. They might create flyers used to advertise school events. They can arrange furniture, hang appropriate posters, and adjust the lighting in the church youth room to make the atmosphere inviting.

Picture-smart children might mature spiritually by picturing Christ with them. For example, how would He prepare for the math test if He were taking it? How might He react if He were on a losing football team? How would He interact with His piano teacher?

You can help your children use their visualization strengths as they apply spiritual disciplines. For instance, if you want your children to take self-examination more seriously, maybe you could describe it as open-heart surgery. They can look around in their heart for any black or shadowy areas.

Encourage your children to picture themselves entering into God's presence when they confess. Ask them if they can describe God's body language and facial expressions as they enter into His presence. Was He happy to see them? Did He change in any way as they confessed?

Reading a Bible translation like *The Message*, that reads more like a story than other translations, may motivate and help picture-smart children mature in their faith. So might the *Amplified Bible*, because it includes more than one acceptable translation of the original Greek and Hebrew words. These additional words and phrases can increase the number of detailed visuals as children read, listen, and study. For example, here's how the *Amplified Bible* translates Philippians 4:6–7: "Do not fret or have any anxiety about anything, but in every circumstance and in everything, by prayer and petition (definite requests), with thanksgiving, continue to make your wants known to God. And God's peace [shall be yours, that tranquil state of a soul assured of its salvation through Christ, and so fearing nothing from God and being content with its earthly lot of whatever sort that is, that peace] which transcends all understanding shall garrison and mount guard over your hearts and minds in Christ Jesus."

If you're not very picture smart, it might surprise you to learn that the physical space picture-smart children use for their quiet times may be important to them. They'll be distracted without the right visual atmosphere. They might want the area lit a certain way or decorated with a particular color. It's also relevant to consider the visual atmosphere where you typically hold family devotions and discussions.

These children may also want their church sanctuary to include elements of art and design. Awhile ago, I taught many parents about multiple intelligences. We met in a large sanctuary with tall and empty side walls. The colors were dull. About half the audience indicated that the lack of beauty was distracting and troublesome to them. I imagine many children would have told me the same thing.

Careers

What might picture-smart children best succeed at after graduating from high school? What might be fulfilling? Two or three other intelligence strengths will strongly influence this. For instance, if they're picture and body smart, they may want to investigate careers that involve their eyes and large- and/or small-motor skills (e.g., cartographer, construction worker, book illustrator, clothing designer, and photographer). A nature-smart strength might combine with picture-smart skills so that urban planning, horticulture, landscape architecture, and navigating appeal to these children.

Another factor is whether their picture strengths are color, art, design, or diagrams. Consider how these differences will influence the following career possibilities: art teacher, geometry teacher, engineer, sculptor, interior designer, movie or video game producer, pilot, surveyor, fashion designer, or window dresser.

BELONGING: WHO WANTS ME?

Children might best meet their need for belonging through attending movies or craft shows or visiting art museums with other picture-smart children. They might also enjoy playing video games together. How about walking in the city to enjoy and comment on architecture, shadows, colors, and the like?

Many picture-smart girls and some boys enjoy scrapbooking. If their mothers enjoy it, too, this can strengthen their relationship. Girls may enjoy shopping and trying on different outfits together. They may experiment with different colors of makeup, unique hairstyles, and new decorations for their bedrooms. They might also be able to advise friends with less picture-smart talent.

This could include giving advice about wardrobe style, where to hang pictures, or how to create a poster assigned by an English teacher. They might take pictures at events and give photo albums as much-appreciated gifts.

The creativity of picture-smart children can add an important and enjoyable dimension to a friendship. So can their sense of humor. Because these qualities can also stress logic- and word-smart peers, picture-smart children must work at getting along with others.

Connecting with God

Since picture-smart children value their creativity, they may connect well to God as their Creator and resonate with Scriptures such as Genesis 1:27; Psalm 51:10; Ephesians 2:10; and Colossians 1:16. They can be very inspired when they understand that they are made in His image, and He is the source of their creativity.

These children think about God with their eyes, just as they think about everything else. Therefore, stained-glass windows, art, jewelry, and movies might draw them to God. Imagine you and your children examining different paintings of the Last Supper or different cross necklaces. Whether done in art museums, stores, or with pictures in books or catalogs, the discussions would be rich!

Descriptive Scriptures might be most engaging for these children. They may find especially appealing and instructive many of the Psalms, accounts of Old Testament heroes and battles, and Jesus' parables, object lessons, and miracles.

SECURITY: WHO CAN I TRUST?

Trusting Things

Depending on other factors, some picture-smart children might tend to put their trust in their ability to look "just right." Perhaps these children trust in their art and design skills, believing they can produce the perfect poster or project. Some of their athletic skill may be due to picture-smart strengths and it can be easy to trust in that. They might develop strengths with video games. They might remember their scores, compare them to others, and place some of their security in beating their friends.

Trusting Parents

Children will more likely trust their parents when their skills and interests are taken seriously. For picture-smart children, this could involve helping them find outlets for their abilities and ways they can further develop their visual skills. This might include trips to art museums, birthday presents of art lessons or art supplies, connecting them with architects and engineers as mentors, making weekly visits to a building site to notice progress and design elements, and volunteering as a family to help paint and decorate a house your church improves for an elderly couple.

Allow your picture-smart children some freedom in arranging and decorating their bedrooms. Ask for their input into which shade of red flowers to plant under the kitchen window; this is another way to respect their gifts. Children of all ages are more likely to trust their parents when they themselves are trusted.

Although it occurred about thirteen years ago, I still vividly recall my dad helping me hang pictures in my new home. He was a successful engineer and he definitely thought with his eyes. He saw things before they were built, possessed an amazing eye for detail, and had unique and beautiful handwriting, just as his father did. I credit all of this to his picture-smartness. I wasn't sure about hanging a framed quote over my couch, but he insisted it would be perfect. He held it where he said it should go. When we measured, we discovered he had held it over the exact center of the couch. That's how fine his eyes worked. To this day, I often smile when I see the quote, because he was right. The colors are ideal and the placement is perfect. I trusted my dad and I'm glad.

You can use rich and descriptive language when disciplining and motivating your children. This will help visuals form in their minds. You can also use pictures and clips from television shows and/or movies. For example, if you're concerned about the disrespect your daughter is showing through her body language, you might find pictures, television clips, and movie scenes to demonstrate your concerns, and the points you're making may be effective. Children will benefit even more by helping you locate them. Comparing the attitudes demonstrated by body language in these pictures and clips may be very instructive. Letting children draw solutions for behavior problems may work, as might having them doodle while you talk with them.

Through the years I've been intrigued by how many children with picture-smart gifts tell me they don't want to look at their parents during difficult discussions. They explain that they may never be able to forget the disappointment in their dad's eyes or the anger in their mom's face, so they'd rather not see it. I encourage you to think about this and ask your children if this might be why they sometimes prefer not to make eye contact with you.

Maybe we shouldn't always command, "Look at me when I talk to you!"

Trusting in God

I believe God frequently communicates with us through our intelligence strengths. Therefore, you may hear picture-smart children declare, "I saw what I'm supposed to do." "God showed me the next step." "I know what to do. I can see myself trying out for first chair!" You need to take these statements seriously and not reject them simply because God may not communicate with you in the same way. Helping children believe in and take these visual promptings seriously is extremely important.

These children may also benefit from being asked to describe and/or draw what they see when praying and worshiping. Giving credence to their minds' visuals is very honoring and will help them trust God. This is also a key when doing family devotions and when they study the Bible on their own. You can ask them, "What did you see as I read that passage?" This may help more than traditional questions like, "What did you learn?" and "What did Jesus do first when arriving at the well?" When studying, if children see Jesus feeding the five thousand men (Mark 6:34–44) or healing Lazarus (John 11:1–44), they may believe more in these miracles, and thus their faith will grow. (I was tempted to put the word *see* from the previous sentence in quotation marks. This would have indicated that they didn't really see Jesus. But I couldn't do this because it diminishes their reality. Many picture-smart children really *do* see Jesus—in their minds!)

ABILITY AND INTEREST?

It's time again to plot your children's abilities and interests. Include your self-evaluation, too, because it should help you understand some of your relationship dynamics. Remember to think about what you learned here *and* what you consistently observe.

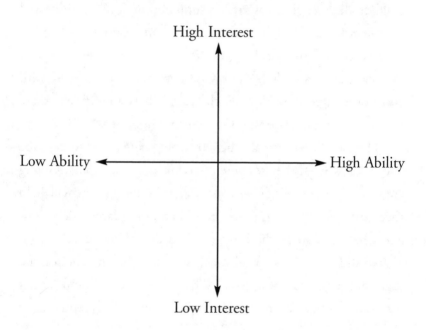

6

I THINK WITH RHYTHMS AND MELODIES...

I AM DEVELOPING MY MUSIC SMART!

"Juan, you're humming and it's bothering the other children. Please stop."

"I'm not humming, Mrs. Roos."

"Juan, you are humming and I need you to stop. And don't start tapping your fingers like you did yesterday. That's distracting, too!"

"I'm sorry! I just don't even know I'm doing it. I always have a song or a rhythm in my head, and I guess it comes out even though I don't want it to!"

"Maybe we can figure out a system I can use to quietly tell you when you're doing it. I know you're musically talented. I can still remember your excellent solo from last month's concert. I want you to keep developing your skills. It's just that you need to remember this isn't music class."

Is that a conversation a teacher might have with one of your children? It might be, if he or she has music-smart leanings. It's also possible that you have a very music-smart son or daughter who doesn't hum or finger-tap. Expression of this smart depends on many factors, including self-control and other intelligence strengths. You'll find out more as you continue reading.

COMPETENCE: WHAT DO I DO WELL?

Music-smart children think with rhythms and melodies, which they're able to hear not only in music, but also in the world around them. Many music-smart children do more than hear music. They appreciate it and analyze it. Children have told me they often don't want to analyze the music, but they can't help themselves. These children often can't study with music on in the background because too much of their attention gets diverted to thinking about the music's composition. Others who are music smart can study better with music on in the background; these children might find it difficult to concentrate in silence.

Music-smart children may enjoy many different musical styles. They may be able to quickly and easily distinguish among composers or styles. Once they've heard a piece of music, they'll often recognize it again. Within the first few measures, these children can tell if a song is jazz or big band. If they're familiar with classical music, they may know if a symphony is by Brahms or Bach.

Producing music is another talent of music-smart children. This may begin when they bang on pots and pans when they're toddlers. If they return to this behavior after you ask them to stop, they may be showing you their music-smart inclination. As you perhaps have discovered, you don't even have to invest in a children's xylophone and tambourines to awaken this smart, although you can. These children may have a good ear and be able to sing in tune. When they're older, their musical ear will help them know if their violin is tuned correctly or if they're playing their trumpet at the right volume. In addition to or instead of playing one or more instruments, they may sing in a choir or perform in school musicals.

I've discovered an interesting intelligence combination as I've traveled to different Asian countries to support missionaries. Some of these missionaries have struggled to learn the language of the people they want to serve because the language is tonal. Though they have word-smart strengths, some of them lack the music-smart ability to hear or create the fine differences in pitch and intonation required to express different meanings of words and phrases in a tonal language. The opposite implication is also clear. Children who are very music smart and word smart may have a special ability to learn tonal foreign languages.

Music-smart children can use their abilities in all types of creative ways. For example, a friend of mine, Kora, teaches children how to make movies on their computers. I know she creates amazing movies of her own, so I e-mailed her to ask which intelligences she uses. I was surprised to discover how important Kora's music-smart strengths are in this process:

> My approach is this: I find the music track that has the mood I am trying to convey with my movie. Then all my movie clips and transitions are dictated by the beat. For example, when I did a Sports Day video for the school, I had the basketball bouncing on

the beat and kids running in slow motion and jumping on the beat.

I noticed my word smart coming into play in my last video. I found a song that reflected what I wanted to say lyrically. I then fit my clips to the words. For example, when the singer sang "from the mountains to the valley" my clip reflected people in the mountains and buildings in the valleys. For "every hand that reaches out" I featured a shot zooming in on hands.

My friend, Rick, is very picture smart. When he makes a movie he still looks for a good sound track, but he doesn't care about the transitions and timing to music. The visual drives everything. (Obviously, video is a visual medium so I still look for a strong visual effect. I just feel that the visual is heightened when transitions are timed to the music.)

My friend, Sunny, is very logic orientated. Her video approach wouldn't work for me. She loads all her clips, works out how long the video is, and then works out how long each clip should be. She gets really mathematical and logical about it.

This is a beautiful example of how intelligences work together. It also demonstrates how we should never quickly assume children can or can't do certain things. For example, you might have assumed that producing movies on the computer depended primarily on your children being picture smart. As we can see from Kora's example, music-smart children can also be successful.

You'll know when your music-smart children are excited because you'll usually hear or see the music they're singing or playing internally. They may tap their fingers or feet to a particular beat or their whole body may shake, rattle, or roll to their internal song. They may spontaneously hum, whistle, or sing because of what's going on in their heart and head. Frequent reprimands to "Stop that noise!" or "Sit still!" can paralyze this intelligence. Of course, so can harsh critiques of their musical practices and performances.

Almost from the time my nieces could talk, they could sing. They responded frequently to life through song. They still do. If Betsy or Katie hears a word, phrase, or Bible verse that reminds her of a song, she will often begin singing. Soon her sister, brother, and parents join in. No wonder we sometimes refer to them as the "Von Koch Family Singers."

Learning and Teaching Methods

To activate children's music-smart attributes, you can use music related to topics they're studying. In history, lessons about the Civil War can be enhanced by playing music from that era. In art, you can play energizing music when you want children to draw quickly and spontaneously. You can also use music to create a certain mood that helps children be more creative. This will help all children because music will activate an intelligence that otherwise might have been ignored in that context. When your child learns and studies with two or more intelligences, he or she will probably do better than if only one is used. You do need to remember, however, that some children can't concentrate with music playing in the background. Therefore, don't play music all the time.

I know of a world geography teacher who teaches the names and spellings of many countries of the world with rhymes and jingles she makes up. I've heard her students sing some of them, and they're very effective. Years later, because many of these young people can still remember the rhymes, they can remember the countries of the world. Another friend, a math teacher, uses a song to help students learn the quadratic formula. Many of us have learned the order of the books of the Bible through a song.

During my assemblies and chapels, when I ask children and teens to say the ABC's, they frequently sing them. They don't *intend* to sing them. They don't *decide* to sing them. The "ABC Song" just comes out. Many laugh. Most of them enjoy finishing the song!

A similar thing occurs when I ask children to spell "Mississippi." They spell it with the rhythm that is the same everywhere I go. It's virtually impossible to spell this word without the rhythm. (Go ahead and try it.) The addition of music improves long-term memory. Therefore, we'll probably never forget the ABC's or how to spell "Mississippi."

No matter their age, your children can benefit by putting to music things they must memorize. They might be able to use the same rhythm as "Mississippi" and/or the melody of the "ABC Song." They can make up their own rhythm or melody. I often recommend that older students replace the lyrics from their favorite song with what they need to remember. For example, this can work with the order of events for their history test, abbreviations for their science class, and words and definitions for health. They can sing this new "song" aloud while at home and in their mind while taking a test in school.

Young children can use the power of sound and music when learning. For instance, if your son struggles to remember the silent "h" in "whisper," you can have him whisper the "h" when saying the letters aloud as you help him study. He would say all the other letters with normal volume. This unique way to emphasize the "h" can help your son remember it's there.

Sometimes the opposite approach works well, too. If your daughter keeps forgetting the "y" in "gym," you can have her shout the "y" and say the "g" and "m" with her normal voice. Even "daughter" can be spelled that way at home as she's learning it. She can shout the silent "gh." Another successful method can be to use rhythm, like cheerleaders might, so it sounds something like this looks: d au gh ter.

Clapping can work, too. When studying addition facts, young children can clap and recite the problem orally: 2 (clap, clap) + 2 (clap, clap) = 4 (clap, clap, clap, clap). This nicely combines several intelligences. They're using word smart because they're talking and listening, logic smart because they're adding, music smart because there will be a rhythm to their clapping, and body smart because they're moving. Although it's not good to overdo it, sometimes the more intelligences, the better!

If you want to further develop your children's music-smartness, you can attend concerts with them, listen to and talk about a variety of musical styles, talk with musicians, and encourage your children to learn an instrument and/or sing in a choir. Some children will take piano lessons for just a year or two. They might ask to stop taking lessons, or their disinterest may make it obvious that their lessons should be discontinued. Even if they quit, that hasn't been time or money wasted. Trust that the investment has awakened and broadened their music-smart intelligence.

IDENTITY: WHO AM I?

Music-smart children might answer the "Who am I?" question by talking about how much they enjoy praising God in song. They might talk about a new musical group, their favorite CD, the best concert they've ever attended, and their musical talent or interest. They might describe the music they're practicing for their next orchestra, band, or choir concert.

Asking them to play or sing a song honors them. Although my own nieces and nephew would sometimes shrug their shoulders when their parents suggested they play or sing for their grandparents and me, I think they secretly enjoyed it. That's certainly how they responded by the time they were finished with their songs. I also know they enjoyed having us at their recitals and concerts. Of course, it has been important to also pay attention to and celebrate their academic pursuits and athletic achievements.

Struggles

Music-smart children may fall into pride in their musical skills, performances, and understandings. If they participate on worship teams, they may believe their public service to God is more important than the service some people do behind the scenes. This is another type of pride. In addition, some music-smart children may look down on others who don't participate in or enjoy music.

There's also the tendency to perfectionism. They may be very hard on themselves when they make a mistake and find it hard to forgive themselves. Paralysis can set in when others are hard on them. High standards that are realistic are appropriate. So is allowing for mistakes and growth.

Music-smart children may make noise when they shouldn't, by finger- and/or foot-tapping, by humming or singing; and they may play their music louder than others prefer. If they're asked to stop and they don't, this disobedience can negatively influence relationships with family members, friends, and teachers.

Some children may cross over from enjoying music to actually idolizing music and/or artists they enjoy. Listen closely to your children. The more you hear them talk about "loving" their music, the more concerned you might want to be. Asking them how much time they spend with God versus listening to their music might be an effective way to begin the conversation. You can also ask if any of their music doesn't edify God, and what they should do if it doesn't.

PURPOSE: WHY AM I ALIVE?

Showcasing God

I grew up in church, attending Sunday worship services with my family and going to Sunday school, vacation Bible school, and church camp like many other children. I still have vibrant memories.

When I was twelve years old, I played "How Great Thou Art" as a viola solo during a worship service. I practiced hard and remember being inspired when it dawned on me that the lyrics were true. I'm confident that I didn't decide to play a solo in church in order to glorify God. I'm sure it had more to do with my developing talent and my teacher's desire that I have a reason to practice diligently. Still, because I was developing and using a talent God chose for me, I believe He was glorified. Anytime we demonstrate God's wiring of us in healthy ways, He is glorified, or put on display.

Music-smart children can choose to glorify and serve God through their singing and instrumental performances. Their motivations are important to God. Do they want to play or sing without error so they look good, or do they want God to look good? Do they whine about practicing and complain to their parents during the week, but then act on a Sunday morning as if they're thrilled to lead people into God's presence? Do they glorify Him during the service, but not while they practice? Gently remind them that God pays attention to it all.

I think music-smart children glorify God by developing their talents through practice. He is also glorified when they humbly take direction from you, their music directors, private teachers, and members of their group.

God can also be magnified when music-smart children believe in their talent and musical joy enough to reject some feedback. Jessie did that. She knew she could sing. She also knew it was a gift from God. People had affirmed her often. Yet her church's new worship pastor didn't choose her for his team. Feedback he provided didn't ring true, and Jessie believed it was a personal issue rather than a question of her talent. Although she went through a very challenging time of self-doubt, she listened to God's affirmations and believed she had singing talent. She didn't give up. After her family changed churches, she observed that church's worship style and leader. She believed she was a good fit, so she auditioned to join one of the worship teams. They selected her! In addition to leading in worship, she is now a part of small ensembles and she occasionally sings duets. Believing in her musical gift and being obedient to God's leading resulted in many being blessed.

God is glorified when any of us studies Scripture, so you'll want to find ways to get children interested. Help your music-smart children locate passages that relate to music and worship.

Studying those passages and some Psalms that were originally sung can bear much fruit (e.g., Psalm 4; 33; 95; and 98; Luke 4:8; 15:25; Ephesians 5:19). It will help them worship "in spirit and in truth" (John 4:24), which is important to music-smart children.

Worship is the spiritual discipline that will probably come easiest to music-smart children. When they worship privately, deep in their heart, God is especially glorified. When they enter into His presence to let Him know what they believe about Him, He is pleased. Sometimes it's during worship that music-smart children are comforted and convicted.

You could encourage music-smart children to find music to play occasionally in the background for your family discussions and devotional times. Better yet, tell them the devotional topic (e.g., God's strength, bearing one another's burdens, or faith) and ask them to find a song to play at the end, as a reflection time.

Careers

Music-smart children can use their abilities and interests in several careers. They can become music therapists, worship pastors, music teachers, composers, conductors, music arrangers, music producers, soloists, and owners of music/instrument stores. They can become jingle writers, advertisers, disc jockeys, and piano tuners. They can help to design Web sites and streaming video that use music effectively, as my friend Kora did.

Perhaps your music-smart child would enjoy a career related to movies and television shows. He or she could be a music editor, sound effects editor, sound engineer (for live performances, too), or a sound designer.

BELONGING: WHO WANTS ME?

I'm writing this chapter while spending some time at my mom's. Tonight, with two friends, she went to a Milwaukee Symphony Orchestra concert. She came home a few minutes ago, beaming as she told me about the outstanding cellos in one of the selections. She provided me with several details and told me about conversations she and her two friends had on their way home from the Wilson Center. Music connects people.

My mom's enjoyment of music began in her childhood. She began taking piano lessons before her family owned a piano. She and her sister practiced on a piece of cardboard designed like a piano keyboard and placed on a table. My mom was selected for the a cappella choir when she was in high school, and she joined the church adult choir when she was just sixteen. My dad began playing the trumpet when he was in junior high school and continued playing through his adult years.

Because music was a part of my parents' lives and they believed it was important, they arranged for my brother, Dave, and me to learn instruments when we were young. We both played the piano, Dave played the trumpet, and I played the viola in the orchestra and the keyboard and rhythm instruments of the percussion section in the band. We both have vivid memories of our high school and college experiences.

I think music can provide a powerful bond in families. I know it did for my brother, my parents, and me. Beyond that, my four cousins on my mom's side are also music smart. Several of us were in junior high and high school band and orchestra together. We formed a unique ensemble when we played for our grandparents' fiftieth and sixty-fifth wedding anniversary parties. Dave was on the trumpet, Terry on sax, Jane on French horn, I was on the viola, Ann played the clarinet, and Nancy played the flute. When my brother married Debbie, she joined us on the piano. Our junior high band director was nice enough to arrange some of my grandparents' favorite songs for our rather strange combination of instruments. We actually sounded quite good. Can you close your eyes and hear us playing "The Waltz You Saved for Me"? I can—music creates vivid memories.

The family tradition continues with Betsy, Katie, and Andy. They, too, have worked to develop their God-given talents. Betsy's first trumpet was my dad's—the same one her dad learned on. She then passed it on to Andy. Katie chose the flute. All three also play the piano and handbells, and two of them have sung in honors choirs. Their mom is a music teacher by profession and still very active on the piano and glorifying God with her trained and beautiful voice. Dave still plays the trumpet in worship bands.

Music serves as a powerful bonding agent between people, providing something to talk about and an emotional experience to share. Music can be enjoyed and experienced for a lifetime, as evidenced by my mom's outing tonight, at eighty years old.

Some music-smart children struggle to relate to peers who aren't interested in music. In addition, unless they're also logic smart, conversations about very practical and logical things often bore them quickly. Some music-smart children tell me that just taking the time for friendship is difficult because of the amount of practice and number of rehearsals they must attend. For these reasons, many music-smart children find their friends within their music groups.

Connecting with God

I'm sure it won't surprise you that most music-smart children will connect with God through praise and worship (e.g., 1 Chronicles 16:9; Psalm 98:9). Whether they're self smart or people smart may influence whether they find individual or corporate worship most fulfilling.

Some music-smart children will study and reflect upon the lyrics of traditional hymns and modern praise choruses. Those who have word-smart strengths may then find Scriptures that support the songs. I also know music-smart children who have enjoyed learning about the lives of composers.

A church that prioritizes worship will be important to music-smart children. Especially if they're mature, they'll want members of worship teams to be talented, but also to be more concerned with leading others into worship than with their own performances. Like my brother and his family, they might prefer miked worship leaders, an orchestra, frequent special music, and a variety of musical styles represented. The quality of music during youth and children's events is an important consideration, too.

SECURITY: WHO CAN I TRUST?

Trusting Things

Music-smart children need to guard against the temptation to trust in their musical abilities and the quality of their performances. Evidence they've done this can be found in how they feel and react when they make mistakes in concerts or recitals. If they're "in a funk" for a long time, talk with them about their security.

Trusting Parents

When you're truly open to hearing why your children like the music they like, they will trust you more. Ask to listen to their music with them. Ask them why certain songs speak to them. You might be pleasantly surprised at what they gain from lyrics you think are shallow. Of course, you'll definitely have standards and draw the line at what music they're allowed to listen to. They may never thank you, but that shouldn't matter.

Your children will also trust you when they see you as a resource to develop their musical interests and abilities. Take them to concerts to introduce them to the beauty of skilled musicians playing together. Do the same with musical theater and large choirs. Watch music specials on television and rent or purchase DVDs of concerts. Encourage your children to choose an instrument to learn and/or to develop their vocal abilities. Buy them what they need. Provide private lessons, if you can, so they can develop more of their talent.

Get to know middle school and high school directors and which instruments they need in their bands and orchestras. Have your children evaluated to see which instruments might be best. If you find out they could play the French horn, trumpet, or trombone, and there are fewer French horn players in the junior high, you might want to recommend that instrument. Be an advocate for them with their music teachers and church worship leaders.

Support both your children's practices and performances. I'm often asked what I think my parents did right to raise two well-rounded children with PhDs who are devoted to God, involved in church, healthy, and generally doing very well in life. One of the first answers I provide is that my parents were genuinely interested in what we did. They enjoyed what we pursued, they had confidence in us, and they communicated that confidence. Dave and I knew we could accomplish just about anything!

Our parents didn't just attend our concerts and recitals, clapping and taking pictures. They made sure our grandparents and great-aunts knew about our concerts so they could attend, too. They paid for and took us to private lessons. They sacrificed and provided for us. To encourage us to practice, they sat in the living room with us at times. They provided helpful feedback. They cared about our efforts that resulted in our performances. I believe this is essential. I recommend you invest in the process that leads your children to the product you hope they achieve.

Trusting in God

Because I'm music smart, God will often meet my needs through song. He did this with "How Great Thou Art" when I was twelve years old. I can't tell you how many times on a Sunday morning, one of the songs my pastor chose was a song I needed to sing. It might have been about following God, and I had been struggling to do that. Just this past Sunday, we sang a song with the lyric, "It's all about You, Jesus." God ministered to me through that simple phrase, and I made an important decision because of the truth confronting me. This is how God works with music-smart people. Teach this to your music-smart children so they understand it's not a coincidence when God meets a need or answers a prayer with a song (Psalm 32:7; Psalm 40:3; Psalm 69:30).

I sometimes whistle. It's completely spontaneous. I don't think, *I haven't whistled in a while. I think I'll whistle!* I just hear myself whistling. I might be in a hotel room, my office, my home, or even walking into a grocery store. I learned a long time ago that whistling is my music-smart self responding to my internal peace. When I realize I'm whistling, it's God saying, "Kathy, pay attention to your peace." It's a beautiful thing! Teach your children to pay attention to these types of occurrences. They need to see God active in their lives!

ABILITY AND INTEREST?

Now it's time to consider what you learned in this chapter and what you observe in your children and yourself. Put it all together and place your name and the names of your children on this graph where you believe they belong. Then strategize, perhaps with them, if change is warranted.

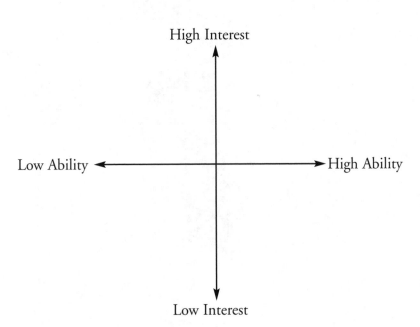

7

I THINK WITH MOVEMENT AND TOUCH...
I AM DEVELOPING MY BODY SMART!

At the beginning of chapter five, I shared part of a letter from Maddie. She wrote it after hearing me teach about the intelligences. She learned that day that she was both picture smart and body smart, and God used the seminar to heal her of some misunderstandings and doubts.

When Maddie was a senior in high school, a guidance counselor told her she would never graduate from college. She enrolled in a nearby college anyway because her parents wanted her to. In her letter to me, she wrote, "I didn't expect to graduate. After all, college was for smart kids who like to study."

Maddie chose to major in theater because of her positive high school theater experiences. Drama combined both her picture- and body-smart strengths. She was able to picture how selected costumes and sets would enhance a particular play. She was able to use her body to effectively mimic a tottering elderly lady or to portray a middle-aged tired woman when those were her assigned parts. I thank God for leading her to college and to this major, and am glad that she did not follow the advice of her guidance counselor. Without her parents' support, I'm afraid she might have.

Maddie graduated from college with a higher GPA than she ever had in high school. Not only that, she also earned a master's degree, graduating magna cum laude. She included this in her letter to me: "I was just short of bursting at the seams with joy and pride. It was so rewarding to obtain a second degree, with honors —especially after being told that I would drop out."

Here's what she wrote next:

> I've had a busy thirteen years since graduating from high school. I feel satisfied with the path my career has taken me: performing in four summer seasons across the nation, working within Walt Disney World's creative costuming department, choreographing professionally in four different states, and touring the nation and Canada as a puppeteer and dancer with an internationally acclaimed performance group. I tell you all of this to drive the point home. There are lots of words I would use to describe myself. Accomplished—yes; successful—yes; assertive, driven, hardworking, talented, creative, determined, gifted, well-educated, and informed —yes. But, up until [attending your workshop], I never would have used the word "smart" to describe myself. I didn't know that the reason I am good at theater is because I am smart. I just thought it was because I am skilled and assertive and eager to work hard on something that interests me.

I know it must sound contradictory to have made it through two degrees and not consider myself smart. But students outside my field in college constantly asked, "Are you taking any *real* classes this semester?" It made me realize the rest of the world thought that what I'm best at took no brain power. So it became easy to believe that while some people are smart, others are talented, and it became even easier for me to turn green with envy when I saw someone who appeared to be both.

I've known for years that I was gifted in more than one avenue in theater—performing, directing, costuming, choreographing, etc., but I really seriously thought that God gave me a well-rounded package to make up for the fact that He didn't make me smart. I can't tell you how freeing it is to find out that *I am smart*, that my abilities come from a God-wired part of my brain!

I fear for kids like me, not because of how they are smart, but because of how people respond to how they are smart.

I wonder how you're reacting to Maddie's statements. Perhaps you can relate because of your own past or your child's strengths or struggles. If not, I imagine you know someone who shares similar experiences to Maddie's. The word *smart* is empowering. I encourage you to use it! The following information will help you know when to do just that.

COMPETENCE: WHAT DO I DO WELL?

Body-smart children think by moving and touching. Motion is very important to them. They learn and think with their entire bodies. Their hands are busy "talking," building, writing, touching, twisting hair, playing, etc. Their feet are busy tapping, shifting in place, or walking. Body-smart children are often moving—sometimes purposefully and intentionally, sometimes not. This is because when body-smart children are excited, they can't help but move. Their bodies often seem to follow the old cheer, even when they're not in the football stands: *Sway to the left—sway to the right—stand up—sit down—fight, fight, fight!* Being in motion is like breathing to body-smart children.

When your son's brain is able to tell his nerves and muscles what to do so that he quickly, accurately, and appropriately moves, he is demonstrating that he is body smart. These children know the power of movement.

Because body-smart children can control their entire body, they usually have strengths with large-motor tasks. Therefore, they may enjoy and be successful at physical pursuits like hiking, sports, dancing, acting, camping, and/or playing musical instruments.

Often body-smart children can also easily execute small-motor tasks. Their eye-hand coordination allows them to handle objects skillfully and to master skills using the finer muscles of their fingers and hands. Small muscle movements are needed for such skills as sewing, carpentry, model building, cooking, and typing.

It's possible to have strengths in large-motor areas but not in small-motor skills, or vice versa. Logically, children with abilities and interests in both are more body smart than children with strengths in just one area. If this intelligence hasn't been awakened yet, however, it's hard to identify strengths with either large-motor or small-motor tasks. If this is true for one or more of your children, I trust you'll make it a priority to activate it soon.

My body smart was awakened because of a wise decision my parents made when I was about six years old. Until then, I had obviously used my body to walk, run, play, color, print, cut, etc. Nevertheless, not unlike many children, I was somewhat clumsy. My parents enrolled me in dance class, and God used the tap and ballet instruction to establish connections between my brain and my body. Because of that class, I overcame my clumsiness. I'm grateful my parents didn't just assume I was destined to be clumsy. Rather, they were solution-focused problem solvers.

Learning and Teaching Methods

When children with body-smart strengths are allowed to move purposefully, they'll have less need to move in disruptive ways. You read that correctly—movement is a *need*. Expecting body-smart children to sit still and keep their hands still for long stretches isn't fair or realistic. I believe this expectation and the constant commands to "Sit still!" and "Put that down!" that often accompany it can paralyze children's body smart. A workable solution is to build movement into lessons.

Young children can march to their spelling words, taking one step for each letter. This won't hurt any student, and it will especially help those who are body smart. The teacher can lead them during school, and/or children can march when practicing at home. For example, if they do this with the word "Texas" at home and then forget the middle letter when taking their spelling test, they can silently march with their big toes under their desks. This "marching" will help them recall the letter "x." Older students can use the same idea when, for example, memorizing the names of countries and vocabulary for their economics test.

Recently, I met with a mom and her second-grade daughter, Pamela, who is struggling with phonics, spelling, and other word-smart tasks. We have evidence that Pamela is body smart and good with her hands. I suggested that she practice her words and phonics patterns (e.g., ain [train, gain], oat [goat, throat], eat [treat, beat]) at home using skywriting. This involves her "writing" her letters and words as large as she can make them in the air with her hand, as if she's holding her pencil. Skywriting also works well when learning chemical formulas, an explorer's name, or a cursive letter. As an alternative to skywriting, I explained that Pamela can use large pieces of chalk on the driveway, wet sponges on chalkboards, and markers on whiteboards.

Because skywriting involves muscles in the fingers, arm, shoulder, and back, it's better for body-smart children than simply writing on paper. Muscle movement helps body-smart children learn and remember. Teachers can lead groups of children in this worthwhile activity in class and encourage them to study this way at home. I recommend that children also say what they're writing, because then they'll be using two more components of word-smart intelligence—speaking and listening—along with the word-smart skill of writing and the body's large-motor actions.

Body-smart children should have clipboards available for their use because they'll have the freedom to pace and study, go sit outside for a while, and sprawl out on the floor in the den where they can freely kick their legs in the air. They may also benefit from reading and studying in rocking chairs and beanbag chairs because these chairs provide the freedom to move. Even "studying" while emptying the dishwasher, cutting the grass, and washing the car may help. Of course, they won't be holding a textbook, but they can rehearse a poem they're memorizing, verbalize the order of events they're studying for their history test, or think through a paper they're writing. Have you ever had a great idea while driving, putting groceries away, or walking upstairs? If you have, that's your body smart at work. This is precisely why these children should not be expected or required to always sit still. It's counterproductive and unrealistic for the way God wired them. (When it's essential, because of others, that they sit still, they must learn to use their self-control to be obedient.)

Learning through drama and role-play can also be effective. It doesn't have to be involved and complicated. For example, if children are learning the difference between shocked and scared, having them make the facial expressions that go with each word can help. When teaching children about Daniel and faith, I remind them of Daniel's strong faith in his great God and that he was in a den with lions. I have the children rise, and I explain that on the count of three I want them to stand as they think Daniel stood among the lions. Some just stand casually, some take a worship posture, and others kneel or position their hands to pray. It's impressive what they do! As the lesson continues, I ask them how *they* think *they* would have stood if *they* had been in the den. I then count to three and have them picture in their minds what they would have done. Their facial expressions tell me that they saw themselves and are thinking about their stance.

Because body-smart children think and learn by touching, it makes sense to use manipulatives. Bending colorful pipe cleaners into letters and numbers may work well. Writing with a finger in dry jello or sand poured into a pan can be effective. Giving children relevant objects to explore and examine can be very motivational and instructive. Remember, they think with their hands, so actually handling an old beehive could do more for them than a ten-minute lecture about it.

Many of the ideas I've just shared are used by teachers of young children, in part, because they don't expect their students to sit still for long periods. Maybe some children do very well in school initially only to have motivation and grades decline as they age because their body-smart strengths are honored only when they're young. I'm always enthusiastic when I meet teachers of older children who have worked to implement activities that help their body-smart students concentrate and learn. These teachers impress me because I know it's not always easy.

The challenge for body-smart children is to exercise self-control, self-respect, and respect for others so they don't move or touch in distracting ways. They need to learn not to do anything that prevents their teacher from teaching or other children from learning. They must sit still and put things down when they're asked to. Obedience is right. Intelligence strengths are no excuse for disobedience. All children must learn to be smart with their smarts—using them to help and not hurt!

Children with body-smart strengths will often drum their fingers, tap their feet, constantly play with something in their hands, or simply find a way to move somehow. You have probably noticed that asking them to stop is only a temporary solution. Their body reacts to truth with movement, so they need to find ways to move that are respectful. (If they drum their fingers or tap their feet to a certain beat, it's usually because they're also music smart.)

If your children drum their fingers on the table while you're talking with them, and it's distracting, you can show them how to use an alternative behavior. I teach these body-smart children to drum their fingers on their thigh, under the table or their desk. Initially, it's not as satisfying because it doesn't make noise, but they can choose to learn to be satisfied. Here's another example. When the movement or noise of their tapping foot is distracting to others, they can choose to tap their big toe to the beat in their mind. They can choose to learn to be satisfied by this smaller and silent movement. That's the key. We can all "choose to learn to be satisfied."

Children who don't have body-smart strengths can benefit from the suggestions I've included here. These children need opportunities to develop both the small muscles in their fingers and hands and the large muscles of their arms and legs. The best way to do this is in a safe environment. Helping them at home, for example, by kicking a ball with them in the backyard, helping them print their letters on a chalkboard or whiteboard, and making things from clay can help. So can enrolling them in dance lessons, as my parents did for me.

IDENTITY: WHO AM I?

After hearing me teach about this intelligence, many children share that they never knew moving well was a way of being smart. I find great joy in helping these children redefine themselves as "smart." Although this intelligence doesn't get the same respect in school that word and logic smart do, children with large-motor and/or small-motor skills *are* smart. One of my fond memories after an assembly is of a high school boy who came up to me and declared: "I'm not a dumb jock. I'm a smart one!"

Body-smart children definitely know who they are. Many of

them are told all day to "Sit down!" and "Put that down!" They admit to me that they are movers, shakers, rattlers, and rollers. I encourage them to find ways to keep this energy from getting them into trouble and to use it in creative and helpful ways. I smiled broadly when a child left a school assembly saying, "I am body smart and I will be smart with this smart!"

Perhaps you've already thought of this: Many children suspected of having Attention Deficit Hyperactivity Disorder (ADHD) may be body smart, *not* ADHD. This disorder and the smart have things in common—moving and learning by touching and direct experiences—so one can be disguised as the other. Many children who have been properly assessed and diagnosed as having ADHD may *also* be body smart. If this is your son or daughter, I encourage you to choose to see his or her physical energy and the ways he or she embraces life through touch and action as strengths. Although proper medication is sometimes appropriate, we must be careful to not medicate out of these children the greatest channel God has given them through which to experience life. I tell children that I'm not so concerned with whether they have ADHD or not, but that they choose to respect others and be self-controlled regardless.

Struggles

Children who are good at using their bodies might be tempted to use them to hurt others and to get themselves into trouble. When young, they may express their frustrations and fears with their bodies, by punching, kicking, pinching, or biting. They might choose to shove their way to the front of the line just because they can. They might enjoy wrestling for fun with parents, siblings, and friends, but then not know when or how to stop before getting too aggressive or dominating the "fight." Again, teaching them to "be smart with their smart" will both affirm their strength and help them develop needed self-control.

PURPOSE: WHY AM I ALIVE?

Showcasing God

All children need to know why they are alive. Although they may not directly verbalize this need, it shows up in questions such as, "Why do I have to do this?" or "What does this have to do with me?" and "What do you think I can do when I grow up?"

These questions may be especially common among body-smart children, because they often feel as though they don't fit in at school, church, or even at home. All of life can feel irrelevant to them. As you now know, they experience life through movement and can't help but move when they're excited. Sitting still isn't easy for them, yet it's almost always expected. Because they often feel unsuccessful, hopelessness and self-doubt can set in. Believing they have a purpose to fulfill is a stretch for them.

Constantly demanding that these children sit, listen, and learn in ways that aren't their strengths can lead to more than hopelessness and a lack of purpose. It can paralyze this smart. Once that happens, body-smart children may not move at all. Apathy creeps in and destroys whatever belief they had. Learning at school and church will be even harder because now they can no longer use one of their greatest strengths. Glorifying God becomes harder, too, if this smart is paralyzed. We need to choose to be optimistic and positive when parenting and teaching these children!

We can teach children how sitting still and listening attentively glorifies God. We can let them know that God understands this is a challenge for them, and He is therefore especially pleased when they work to control their need to move. Discovering they can be physically quiet can give these children great hope. What's the key? You need to find the stamina and character to be positive and optimistic while you help them learn the self-control they need. There's a big difference between asking them to sit still and teaching them to sit still. *You* glorify God when you teach. This can include your role modeling of appropriate behavior. You can also specifically compliment your children when they are sitting still. Rather than telling them they're "good," which doesn't teach them what to continue doing, use specific language such as, "Thank you for not swinging your legs or twisting your hair. You did nothing to distract me or anyone else. You are learning self-control."

There's more that body-smart children can do. God is glorified when children develop their large-motor and small-motor skills and use them to point people to Him. Children can worship and serve God through interpretive dances that might also bless another's worship experience. Body-smart children can also learn sign language so they can interpret for the deaf during church services and conferences. Or they might form or join a church drama team to minister during church or youth services. Puppetry and clowning come easily to many body-smart children. They may enjoy using these skills to present evangelistic programs for younger boys and girls. Creating three-dimensional art might be another outlet for body-smart children. Other smarts that are strengths will influence these decisions.

Athletes can demonstrate Christlikeness on church-sponsored

or school teams, or when helping to coach younger children's sports teams. They can also use sports as a platform for evangelism. My niece, Katie, traveled to Northern Ireland to play soccer when she was in high school, and she's heading to South Africa soon with her college team. On these mission trips, she tells athletes on the other teams, "I play for Christ. That's why I play. Why do you play?"

Other activities geared to body-smart youth include joining cheerleading squads or drill teams, playing the drums or a clarinet in the band, neatly printing words on posters created by picture-smart peers, or volunteering to help teachers arrange projects or trophies in a display case.

As you think about glorifying God by raising body-smart children to do the same, remember they experience life through touch and movement. They learn more by *doing* than by listening. Family devotions will be more effective when you plan something for these children to do. Anything that keeps their hands busy will help. Allow them to stand, pace, or wiggle in their chair. Using drama, action, and object lessons in shorter teaching times will help.

Perhaps the best way to involve many muscles, and thus enhance learning, is to have children serve others in some capacity. For example, these children could memorize Bible verses and then do a dramatic reading of those verses at a nursing home. After learning about putting others first, your family could volunteer to serve lunch to the construction team building your church's addition. What examples can you think of that fit your family's interests well?

Careers

Children who are very body smart will probably gravitate toward careers that rely on a sense of touch, hand-eye coordination, and/or large-motor movements. I'm glad my chiropractor is body smart. I stay on the table during my adjustment! I'm glad my dentist is body smart because the drill goes only where the drill belongs. I'm glad Belle, my hairdresser, is very body smart and cuts my hair so that it looks just right on me.

Perhaps your children will enjoy these or any of the following vocations: mechanic, physical education teacher, orchestra conductor, carpenter, plumber, welder, truck driver, stunt person, physical therapist, surgeon, actor, seamstress, sports coach, or camp director.

BELONGING: WHO WANTS ME?

Being wanted is a need every child has. Many body-smart children will meet this need through team sports. Typically, they relate well to other athletes and enjoy the camaraderie, especially if they are also people smart. They may also enjoy watching live and televised sporting events with friends and family members.

Body-smart children might also bond during shop class, as they work in teams to create wood toys for hospitalized children. Of course, the other activities they participate in, such as drama and art, will also influence their feelings of belonging.

It's also possible that body-smart children will be most accepted by other children who move frequently. I notice that those who move and touch a lot often have best friends who are just like them. This is because they bond, at times, through misbehavior. Ideally, they can learn to help each other and even hold each other accountable to make wise choices.

The almost constant motion of some body-smart children can distract and irritate others. For this reason, other children may not choose them as friends. How teachers react to body-smart children and what they tell other children about them influences how strong their sense of belonging will be. If non-body-smart children only see these children as troublemakers, they may choose to ignore them. This is unfortunate, because the high energy and teamwork strengths many of them have could be a blessing rather than an irritation.

Connecting with God

Body-smart children may connect with God best when they move. Being physically involved during worship may be important to them. However, be careful not to judge whether someone is body smart based only on whether they sway, clap, or lift their hands during worship. One of my best friends is very body smart and yet very still as she worships God. She talks with her hands, is a former athlete, exercises regularly, and enjoys rocking chairs; but while worshiping, her body is often still. Others may feel God's presence best when they are standing to worship or kneeling to pray.

Because body-smart children learn by doing and by experiencing things for themselves, ordinances like Communion, baptism, and financial giving can be very important. You may want to attend baptism services, have children put money in the offering plate, and take advantage of Communion as a very important teaching time.

Are there certain Scripture passages that might capture the

attention of body-smart children? That will depend upon which body-smart strengths and interests they have. They might enjoy and benefit from passages about building (e.g., Nehemiah; Luke 6:46–49), running (1 Corinthians 9:24–27; 2 Timothy 4:7), strength in battle (e.g., 1 Samuel 17; Psalm 18), crafts (e.g., Exodus 31:1–11), or whether they can feel themselves putting on God's armor for spiritual battle (Ephesians 6:10–18).

SECURITY: WHO CAN I TRUST?

Trusting Things

Although children need to put their trust in God and trustworthy people, it's common for them to put at least a part of their security in things. Because trusting things is unhealthy, you need to make sure you don't encourage or model this. Body-smart children may be tempted to trust their talent or their ability to create art because of their keen eye-hand coordination, to type quickly and accurately because of their finger dexterity, or to jump quickly over hurdles at a track meet.

An unhealthy trust in body-smart abilities may surface as an inordinate *need* to win at games or in contests. Be concerned if your son is playing on a soccer team, entering sculptures in art contests, or learning the bass guitar to earn a position on a worship team all in order to win. This may be how he feels validated as a person. The *need* to win can change a fun wrestling match with a brother into an aggressive, competitive, out-to-win-at-any-cost match.

After a tennis match or basketball game, if the first question you ask is, "Did you win?" your children will assume that winning is most important to you. Winning may then become most important to them, and they'll only feel good about themselves when they win. What might happen if the first questions after the game are "Did you have fun? How Christlike were your attitudes? How Christlike were your actions?"

Trusting Parents

Body-smart children will trust you when you view their energy and need for action as positive qualities. In contrast, children will distance themselves from parents who are easily frustrated and who constantly tell them to sit down, sit still, and keep their hands quiet.

Children pay attention to and trust parents who help them develop their body-smartness through lessons, practicing in the backyard, spending time on relevant activities, and by providing needed materials for their use. This is especially true when children and parents play a sport together and work together on projects, such as changing the oil in a car and sweeping out the garage. I imagine there are many parents and children who can testify to bonds formed in the swimming pool or on the golf course. Children may talk more during these body-smart times and thus increase their sense of belonging. Belonging and trust go hand in hand.

Considering body-smartness when disciplining and motivating children means you will let them move respectfully during serious talks. Ask them to act out solutions rather than simply talking about them. Even practicing proper behavior—like walking rather than running in the kitchen—may help, as long as the practice isn't overdone or assigned in a demeaning way.

Remember these children learn through touch. Therefore, use touch-praise and touch-correction judiciously. When you want to compliment a child who is body smart, pat him on the back, tussle his hair, and make eye contact while you speak the affirmation. The same is true when you need to offer helpful correction. Gently touch your daughter's wrist when you talk with her about her need to put things down the first time you ask. Gently grip your son's head or touch his forehead when you talk with him about his need to slow down and think more carefully about what he is doing. These physical connections may help your children remember your words.

Trusting in God

Just as picture-smart children need to learn to trust the pictures God gives them, body-smart children should be encouraged to trust their gut reactions and physical responses. They may talk about feeling certain they shouldn't go to a concert or that they should call their grandmother. They might also talk about "being moved" to do or say something (Genesis 43:30; Exodus 35:21).

Remember my earlier illustration where I ask children to picture themselves standing as if they had been in the lion's den with Daniel? Numerous children have told me that's been a more effective way for them to judge the depth of their faith than anything else they've experienced. Regularly using body-smart activities with children allows them to fully experience and trust God.

ABILITY AND INTEREST?

What body-smart abilities and interests do you and your children have? Could differences be a source of conflict? Are your relationship strengths due, in part, to your commonalities? As you plot your names, think about what you learned here and what you've observed through the years.

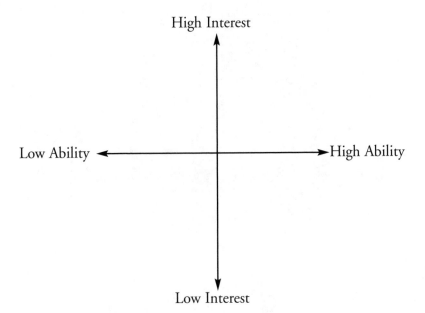

8

I THINK WITH
PATTERNS...
I AM DEVELOPING MY NATURE
SMART!

My niece, Betsy, is definitely someone who can declare, "I am nature smart!" Her dad remembers her being more interested in stuffed animals than dolls or other toys from the time she was a toddler. When she did play with dolls, it was usually to have them ride the little play ponies she owned. When she was just fifteen months old, one of her Christmas gifts was "Brownie," a small rocking horse. She loved it and rode it a lot, most of the time more vigorously than anyone would have expected.

Betsy's natural inclination toward animals meant she was always comfortable around them. When visiting petting zoos, her parents report that she "just seemed to know what to do, with neither fear nor foolish risk." No one taught her any of this.

Rather, these natural tendencies were from God. Her parents noticed and supported them. My parents also supported Betsy's nature-smart interests by holding a zoo membership for years so that Betsy could go often.

Betsy remembers the name of her first pet, a fish named Zebra. In addition to other fish, she had two gerbils named Jasmine and Cookie. Then came her beloved dog Snickers. Betsy cared so much about Snickers that she "led" her in a prayer to trust Christ as her Savior. Nature-smart children can be quite serious about this!

Betsy began taking horseback riding lessons when she was young. This possibility never even entered her parents' minds until Betsy suggested it. Other than her rocking horse and toy ponies, they can't imagine where she even got the idea that someone could take horseback riding lessons. This desire was born into her by her Creator God! Betsy enjoyed cleaning Smokey Joe's stall, taking the dirt out of his horseshoes, brushing him, and feeding him. She didn't mind the winter cold, and she loved competing and was never nervous.

I'm proud of my brother and sister-in-law for supporting Betsy's interests. For a while, Betsy's mom gave piano lessons to the daughter of Betsy's horseback riding teacher in trade. When Betsy got a new teacher and entered many 4H contests for riding Smokey Joe and for showing Snickers, her parents trusted God for the necessary funds. They sacrificed for their daughter.

I remember being in the car as we pulled up to Pleasant Hill Farm. Betsy would smell the manure, take a deep breath, and exclaim, "I love this smell!" The rest of us disagreed! I love how God works, though. Through Betsy's inborn nature-smart strengths, many others had their nature-smart intelligence awakened or strengthened. It's never too late! Her parents, my parents, Betsy's sister and brother, and I all became more nature smart because of Betsy's interests and abilities.

Are you raising a child like Betsy? Or would you like to further awaken a child's nature-smart intelligence? Keep your children's strengths, challenges, and interests in mind as you read the rest of the chapter, and you'll determine whether they have high or low nature-smart ability and high or low nature-smart interest.

COMPETENCE: WHAT DO I DO WELL?

Nature-smart children think with patterns. This is how they remember if a bird they see is a bluebird or blue jay. They'll also know if the trees they're walking past are elm trees or oak trees because they remember which has leaves with rounded ends. They pay attention to similarities and differences, so they may remember details about the variety of fauna and flora in their state. (Do you consider yourself word smart, but you're unfamiliar with the words *fauna* [animals] and *flora* [plants]? Perhaps this is because you're not terribly nature smart. Remember—our intelligences don't work alone.)

Nature-smart children use their eyes. Therefore, this intelligence has close ties to picture-smartness. However, nature-smart children don't think with visuals in the same way picture-smart children do. Rather, because they think with patterns, they notice shapes, sizes, colors, designs, and textures in their environment. They easily and naturally think with comparisons and contrasts. They tend to categorize easily. They know there's power in observing patterns.

Children who are nature smart may notice patterns with more than their eyes. They may also use their sense of touch to notice the texture of leaves, the curves in rocks and seashells, and how the temperature of the pond water compares to the temperature of the water in a puddle. This thinking-by-touch relates to being body smart. Do you see the connections?

My mom is able to display flowers in beautiful arrangements. She has a knack for growing flowers, too. She and my dad enjoyed the unique variety of flowers they planted in different parts of our yard. When my parents sold their home and downsized to an apartment, they secured permission to plant flowers around their patio. I don't think they would have moved to that complex without permission to plant. Even though they found it difficult to take care of their gardens, they hated giving them up.

Now, in my mom's second-floor apartment in a different complex, her flower boxes and barrels of geraniums on the balcony are important to her. Her nature-smart strength allows her to put flowers and leaves with varying colors, heights, and textures together in the perfect vase. When I visit her in the summer and fall, her designs greet me in each room of her apartment.

What nature-smart strengths do your children have? Are they already interested in gardening? Are they able to grow plants well even where there's not much rain but lots of sun? Do they like to go with you to help choose which colors of petunias and pansies to plant? Do they choose rocks of ideal size and color for your new rock garden?

Like Betsy, perhaps your children's nature-smart strengths show up more with animals. Maybe they enjoy taking care of classroom pets and have pets of their own. Like me, maybe they enjoy the zoo. Perhaps they collect bugs and don't want you to step on ants or spiders.

Weather can be another area of strength for nature-smart children. They might pay attention to it, learn to accurately predict if a storm is coming, and enjoy watching the clouds. They might also easily remember which are cumulus and which are stratus. Patty, a friend who teaches special-needs children, told me about a student of hers who reads poorly and can barely add and subtract. Yet as soon as he gets to her room and gets online every morning, he gives the weather report. That is his interest and his ability.

Nature-smart children tune in to their surroundings. According to Dr. Howard Gardner, people raised in cities will use their nature-smart abilities in city environments. Those raised in rural settings will use them in nature. No matter the surroundings, they use the same skills to observe, analyze, and remember the patterns.

Outside, it's the park and remembering where the drinking fountain is. Inside, it's the shadow the setting sun creates when shining on the chandelier. Outside, it's the green and brown pattern on the snake your son just caught. Inside, it's the collection of ceramic and stuffed sheep your daughter arranges just so. Outside, it's the meticulous care your children take when choosing a Christmas tree. Inside, it's the designs in the drapes and the throw pillows that grab your daughter's attention. Outside, it's the search your daughter goes on for exactly the right seashell. Inside, it's your son constantly feeling the texture of his grandfather's African-carved cane.

As with other intelligences, there's a hierarchy of giftedness within nature smart. For example, I enjoy nature. In my travels, I've been privileged to see the snowcapped mountains of Lake Tahoe, fog rolling across the hills of Scotland, and animals during a safari in Senegal, Africa. I appreciate nature; I don't need to understand it. Many children are more nature smart than I am because they want to understand plants, animals, clouds, weather, and all other elements associated with the environment. And many can!

Several years ago, I taught a one-week learning styles course at a seminary north of San Francisco. I had been told deer lived on campus. Instantly, many questions formed in my mind: How did they get here? Why do they stay? What do they eat? Why aren't they hit and killed by cars? Would they prefer to leave if they could?

When coming back from lunch one day with Dr. Williams, the vice president for academic affairs, several deer ran across the road in front of our car. He was able to avoid them. I exclaimed, "What are they doing here?" This question did not spring from being nature smart. That's definitely not one of my strengths. What smart do you think drove the question? It was my logic-smartness. I asked that question because I want things to make sense, and it makes no sense to me that deer live on this busy campus.

I want my example to remind you to avoid trying to determine children's intelligence strengths based on isolated incidents and brief exposure. Dr. Williams might have falsely assumed I was very nature smart. That wouldn't have been terribly serious, of course, but you could negatively affect motivation and learning if you misjudge a child's intelligence strengths, and design learning activities based on that decision. So be careful. Remember to look for consistency.

Allow me to point out something else. If your child asks a question like mine and it seems out of character, it may be your opportunity to help God awaken that intelligence. In other words, if you had been driving the car and your child had asked about the deer, "What are they doing here?" you could have taken the time to help him or her find the answer. You could have asked what other questions your child had. You could have suggested some of your own and then worked together to research the answers. This interaction and the questions' answers might awaken your child's nature-smart part of the mind. Look and listen for these opportunities with each of the eight intelligences. Then choose to take the time to delve in and strengthen your child's intelligences. It will be time well spent.

The naturalist intelligence is perfect for demonstrating another reality I've written about several times. Your child's intelligences never work alone. Many sciences are very related to nature, whether it be plants, animals, landforms, or weather. That's why it's so important to me that we don't allow children to believe or say they're not good at science. That's too general a statement. It might be true that some children have to work diligently to earn acceptable grades in general science. That doesn't necessarily mean they'll struggle in biology the following year.

Some children who struggle with logic-smart sciences like chemistry and physics can be very successful at nature-smart sciences. Which of these might be worth exploring soon? Astronomy (stars and planets), biology (plants and animals), botany (plants), ecology (environment), earth science (earth), entomology (bugs), geology (physical nature and history of earth), herpetology (reptiles and amphibians), horticulture (flowers), ichthyology (fish), meteorology (weather), oceanography (environment of ocean), ornithology (birds), paleontology (fossils), volcanology (volcanoes), and zoology (animals). (Did you notice that this list is in alphabetical order? The logic-smart part of me couldn't help it!) Has your word-smart curiosity been activated? Are you wondering what the word ending "-logy" means? It's a "science, doctrine, or theory of something."

Within history, there may be sections of courses that more easily engage nature-smart children. For example, they may be fascinated by how explorers used the stars for navigation, tracked animals for food, and made canoes with handmade tools. Because, as a people group, Native Americans have obvious nature-smart strengths, a study of them may inspire your children. Remember these and other connections you come up with if you have opportunity to guide your children to choose a topic for a paper they must write. If they're typically not interested in history, but you know they're interested in nature, show them how the two connect. The same can be done in Bible class. For example, if your child needs to choose a denomination to study, perhaps studying the Amish would be a good fit.

Learning and Teaching Methods

To activate the nature-smart part of the mind when studying, children should be encouraged to look for patterns and to notice similarities and differences. This can help when they're studying things such as poetry, Old Testament heroes, prefixes on vocabulary words, and design elements in art class. Learning cursive letters, distinguishing among triangles in a geometry assignment, and remembering formulas in physics can all be made easier when you challenge them to discover patterns.

Nature-smart children usually enjoy collecting and categorizing things by shape, color, design, texture, and such. Therefore, include assignments that ask them to gather specific things. They may enjoy collecting rocks, feathers, leaves, and acorns. They can also collect small, medium, and large things that begin with the letters "br."

Help them find ways to relate what they're studying to nature. This can enhance their motivation, increase their attention, and help them remember the information. For example, when a friend of mine from New Zealand was thirteen, she and her peers needed to choose an industry to study. She chose the guide-dog industry because she loved dogs. (Now she understands that she is very nature smart.) Her peers chose the standard big businesses. She remembers them being bored by the assignment while she loved it.

Studying outside can also help these children. Note, however, that some nature-smart children might find it distracting. Children who want to study outside might need to prove they can finish their assignments efficiently and effectively in that setting.

You can strengthen children's nature-smartness by teaching them how to compare, contrast, and categorize. Use games and activities that help them see patterns. This can be as simple as showing your child several designs and having him identify the two that match. Train their eyes to see details in patterns. You can also create opportunities for them to interact with animals and to investigate something outside. These experiences will be most successful when they have clear and specific purposes. If your children lack confidence, it's especially a good idea to design these nature-smart activities so they can rely on one of their strong intelligences at first.

IDENTITY: WHO AM I?

Children who are interested in nature-smart activities may answer the "Who am I?" identity question with statements like these:

- "I love animals!"
- "I love camping, hiking, and sleeping in tents."
- "I collect rocks. Do you want to see them?"

They may also choose to answer the question for the future:

- "I'm going to be a veterinarian."
- "I'm going to own a pet store."
- "I want to be an animal trainer for the circus."
- "I'm going to be a weather forecaster."

You can also tell if a child has nature-smart strengths by whether he or she talks about wanting to be outside. When I ask for a show of hands during my programs, at least half of each group indicates they'd rather be outside than inside. When they're excited, they really want to go outside. They tell me that being surrounded by nature seems to add to their joy. They may want to just sit on the grass and watch the clouds. They may want to run and play, ride their bikes, kick rocks, shoot hoops, go to a park, sit and watch birds play in the birdbath, or talk to you or someone else while going for a walk or sitting on the front porch. Nature-smart children often care about the environment. They may talk with you about pollution, recycling, collecting litter along highways, and alternative energy sources. Dr. Tom Armstrong has identified these children with the subcategory of "eco-smart." They desire to take care of natural places and living things. They want to protect the environment and preserve it for future generations.

In much the same way as for body smart, nature-smart children will benefit from knowing that their abilities with plants, animals, and the out-of-doors spring from a part of their mind. They can be deeply encouraged to learn that they're not just *good with* animals but they're *smart* because they are.

Nature-smart children can struggle after being inside for long stretches, especially if there aren't windows. Under these circumstances, they may become more irritable and negative than other children. Unless there are indoor pets at home, being inside all the time is also an easy way for this intelligence to be paralyzed, if it had been awakened already. Other things that paralyze nature smart include never being allowed to get dirty outside, never having collections honored, and never creating opportunities for your child who wants a dog or cat to spend time with one.

Struggles

Some children with nature-smart strengths might be tempted to worship the created instead of the Creator. As friends of mine concluded, they might confuse the "awe" of nature for God. I wonder if some children who skip school are nature smart? Huck Finn comes to mind.

PURPOSE: WHY AM I ALIVE?

Showcasing God

My friend Jelina loves dogs. This led her to volunteer at a local animal shelter. She beams when she talks about playing with the dogs there, cleaning their cages, and helping to feed them. It's an obvious source of joy for her. I doubt that she decided to volunteer because she was looking for a new way to glorify God. Rather, she decided she had time to volunteer somewhere, she saw an article about the animal shelter, and she chose it because she realized it matched her interests well. God is glorified by her serving according to the gifts with which He equipped her. I want children to know that they don't have to grow up before they volunteer in similar ways. They can begin now! I hope you tell them that, and I hope you're a role model for them.

Children might help science teachers take care of classroom animals and plants. They might volunteer to water plants in the school office. They could help the busy maintenance staff take care of bushes near the school's front door and flowers by the flagpole. These children might also be the ones who will complain less than others will when you ask them to help you mow your lawn or rake the leaves.

Nature-smart children can serve God by helping to decorate the church sanctuary or youth room with plants and objects with different textures. Like picture-smart children, they might be able to arrange things in an appealing, nondistracting way.

Recycling is a practical way to glorify God. So is looking for lost animals, taking good care of pets, trying not to drive over new grass bordering the driveway, and apologizing if it does happen. When your family takes your gentle dog to visit residents at an assisted-learning center, God is also glorified.

I imagine that many, if not most, missionaries serving around the world in nature-smart ways began developing their interests and abilities in childhood. Do you know missionaries working with farmers to develop hardier crops that will thrive in poor climates? What about missionaries working to plant trees that grow quickly with deep root structures so less ground erodes during floods? How about men and women teaching science in schools for missionary children in foreign lands? Introduce your children to these heroes and help them see that developing their skills now could pay huge kingdom dividends later.

Perhaps you've thought of an important implication for how nature-smart children prefer to approach spiritual disciplines. If given the chance, most will want to read Scripture outside or in a beautiful part of their home that has natural lighting and a view of the yard or a nearby field. They may prefer to pray in similar locations and meet with a Bible study outside when weather permits. Because I'm not very nature smart, this isn't important to me. After interviewing and observing children with nature-smart preferences, however, I understand how important it is for nature-smart children to be outdoors as much as possible. This need might explain why some children don't consistently apply the disciplines when they try to do them in their rooms.

Careers

I've already alluded to several careers in this chapter. Each science discipline has careers associated with it. Every animal shelter needs employees. So do florist shops, Christian camps, and recycling centers. Your children might also want to consider careers like these: tree surgeon, forest or park ranger, veterinarian or veterinarian's assistant, environmental inspector, landscape designer, nature photographer, missionary, and pet sitter.

BELONGING: WHO WANTS ME?

When I checked into a hotel room for a recent event, I discovered a generous gift basket left by the group who hired me to speak. It included a small yellow rosebush. I found out later it was chosen for me because I live in Texas and the florist thought of the song, "The Yellow Rose of Texas." (He or she must be music smart!)

I traveled from that event to a friend's house to work on this book. Upon arriving at Honey's, I told her I'd like to give the plant to her. Without skipping a beat, she said, "I'll let Elisse take care of it." Elisse often stays with Honey when she's in the area, so Honey regularly benefits from Elisse's knowledge of plants, ability to take care of them, and willingness to work in the yard to do what's necessary. Honey herself is extremely nature smart, but she knows Elisse enjoys taking care of the yard. So Honey lets her, honoring Elisse in this way. They're a good team.

Like adults, your children's need for belonging will sometimes be met through children and adults who are like them and sometimes through children and adults who have opposite intelligence strengths. Like Elisse, they might be appreciated for interests and talents that bless others. If your children also like learning, they may enjoy relating to someone who is different from them and who can open new avenues of discovery.

Making friends with nature-smart children usually results in spending lots of time outside and going to parks, zoos, and aquariums. When two or more nature-smart children form a friendship, you can almost always count on them being outside more than inside and dirty from exploring something they discovered. If stuck inside with no nature DVDs to watch or animals to play with, they may struggle unless their other intelligences kick in. For example, if they're also word smart, they may be calmed by reading books about nature or having you read the books to them. If they have logic-smart strengths, exploring nature Web sites together can also be an excellent use of your time. If they're body smart and learn well with their hands, they may enjoy sculpting a volcano out of plaster of Paris. They can use their logic-smart abilities to make it as accurate as possible and their picture-smart abilities to choose realistic paint colors.

Connecting with God

I know a number of adults with definite nature-smart strengths who easily worship God while in the woods or while sitting on a bench overlooking a wooded area. When they hear birds chirping and observe vibrant fall leaves, they immediately think of God's creativity. Some worship well by spending time alone with God, enjoying the trees, clouds, and breeze.

When did these preferences begin? When their nature-smart intelligence was awakened. People whose nature smart was activated in childhood describe rich times with God while at church camps and while walking in the woods with their families. If it was awakened later, they've enjoyed the more recent discovery of how valuable being outside can be to their spiritual growth. If you believe your children have nature-smart strengths, encourage them to connect with God outside and through His wonderful creations.

My niece, Betsy, trusted Christ when she was very young. She was baptized when she was almost eleven years old. Her parents told her they wanted to buy her something meaningful to commemorate her important decision. Betsy asked them to buy and plant a pear tree in the backyard. I never would have thought of that! When my brother changed jobs and the family moved across country, not being able to take the tree with them was one of the difficult realities of the move.

Scripture that God might especially use to draw these children to Himself and to mature them into Christlikeness include the creation story from Genesis 1, the story of Noah (Genesis 6–9), and miracles like the parting of the Red Sea (Exodus 14). Analogies such as the sheep and shepherd and eagle and eaglet can also be very effective. Parables such as the parable of the sower (Matthew 13:1–23) and the parable of the weeds (Matthew 13:24–30, 36–43) will often easily communicate truth to those who are interested in nature. So will the many Psalms that use nature, such as the inspiring Twenty-third Psalm.

SECURITY: WHO CAN I TRUST?

Trusting Things

As with the other intelligences, children who are very nature smart may attempt to put their security in things, such as their ability to understand nature and explain it to others. They may also be tempted to trust in the joy they experience while embracing nature. They'll eventually see that this doesn't work, but they can be hurt in the meantime. Keep alert to whether your children seem to be trusting in things so you can guide them to truth.

Trusting Parents

What did you learn about nature-smart children trusting parents in the story of my niece, Betsy, from the beginning of this chapter? I know she learned she could trust her parents when they responded well to her obvious love of animals and arranged for her horseback riding lessons. I doubt that Betsy is any different from your children. They notice when you listen to them, see what intrigues them, help them answer their questions, explore outside with them, say yes to the things you can, and say no to the things you should.

When having important conversations with nature-smart children, I recommend you remember their love of the outdoors. If possible, talk with them outside, in the backyard, or while you're walking in the neighborhood together. Even choosing a restaurant booth by a window can lead to more productive conversation.

Remember that nature-smart children think with patterns and have strengths in comparison-contrast thinking. You can use this to your advantage when you need to talk about behavior issues. Ask them to compare their current behavior to their past. You can talk about how your current attitudes compare to the attitudes you hold when they're obedient. See if they can identify steps to take to improve what's going wrong before you tell them what you want them to do.

Trusting in God

Children who are very nature smart will more likely trust God when they're encouraged to connect with Him as I described earlier. Teaching them that God is the Creator of the universe may help them trust Him. So will being available to them during and after natural disasters when they may have more questions than children who aren't terribly nature smart. Earthquakes, tornadoes, hurricanes, wildfires, and tsunamis may cause anxiety, concern, and curiosity. You can discuss passages such as Psalm 46, Psalm 107, and Zechariah 10:1 with them. Respecting their questions and statements will help them grow in their ability to trust God.

ABILITY AND INTEREST?

What will your children's nature-smart plots look like? How much interest do they have? How much ability? What about yours? When remembering everyone in your family, make sure to consider what you've learned here and what you've recently observed.

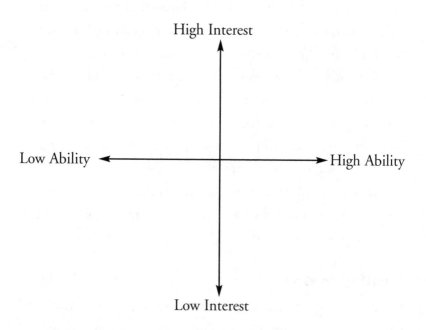

I THINK WITH
PEOPLE...
I AM DEVELOPING MY PEOPLE
SMART!

B randon, are you finished with your homework?"

"Kind of."

"How can you be 'kind of' finished? Either you're finished or you're not."

"I wanted to tell you what I wrote so far and see what you think about it. Remember, you and Mom are the ones who taught me that I think well when I talk out loud. Your questions always help me think. Well, usually they do."

"Okay. You're right. I'm glad we figured out that you're a lot like me in that way."

"Well, anyway . . . I had to come up with a goal for how I want to feel next month, and I had to list things that I think will affect my goal. After praying and thinking about a lot of goals, I chose peaceful.

There's a lot going on and it would be good to have peace in the midst of everything. So could you look at my list of things that might help me feel peaceful and the things that might not? Like, I'm not sure where to put Grandpa's death. You and Mom said he'll probably die soon. I'll miss him, but I'll be glad he's no longer suffering and that he'll be with Jesus. Maybe I won't feel peace right away, but then I will. So do you think I should put it on both lists? Does that make sense? Where would you put it? And I want to ask you about prayer, too. It doesn't always add to my peace. Does it for you?"

If your child regularly wants to talk with you while studying or after studying, this might indicate he or she is people smart. This is the child who asks teachers, "Can I do this with a partner?" This is the child who is often told to stop talking.

Of course, there's much more to being people smart. Let's find out which of your children have these abilities and which ones could afford to have them strengthened.

COMPETENCE: WHAT DO I DO WELL?

People-smart children are interested in people. They tend to make friends easily, partly because they understand people. They people-watch at the mall, at the basketball game, and maybe during math class. Of course, this isn't a wise use of brain power if it means they're not listening to their teacher.

Being people smart involves more than being a good friend, being comfortable with people, or needing people. It involves the definite strength of reading body language. They know if someone is mad, glad, or sad. If your child is able to discern that you're concerned and not angry, or content and not bored, it's because he or she is people smart.

At the high end of the hierarchy of giftedness is the child who can accurately discern someone's mood, intention, and desire *as well as* respond appropriately. For example, as some people-smart children talk, they can discern listeners' reactions by observing changing facial expressions and body language. Have you noticed your son doing this? For example, when he comes to you with a question, do you ever think he's going in one direction, only to have him change his question midstream? Maybe he observed something in your reactions that concerned him. He didn't want you to answer no, so he changed the wording of his question in hopes of getting a maybe or yes response.

This ability can benefit your children in school as well as at home. Picture your daughter paying attention to her history teacher. If she's people smart, she'll be able to determine what content her teacher will stress on the test as his voice, gestures, and body language change during the review. Therefore, she'll know what to study in more depth, and her grade may reflect it. This is just one of many reasons to strategically develop each child's people-smartness.

As the opening anecdote demonstrated, people-smart children think by bouncing ideas off others. This is not only a preference; it's a strength. They think well with others. They admit that sometimes they don't know if their idea is good until they hear themselves say it and watch someone respond to it. I can definitely relate to that. Can you?

Learning and Teaching Methods

Because people-smart children talk when they get excited, they benefit when teachers, tutors, pastors, and parents understand this about them. These children often talk to peers, even when they shouldn't (such as in the middle of class). They may initiate the conversations or eagerly respond if another student talks with them. Often their talking is a spontaneous response to their joy of discovery. Their interactions express high energy; connection is the source of their power.

Just as word-smart children need self-control so they don't talk all the time, so do people-smart children. In fact, if like me, your children's word-smart and people-smart intelligences are both strengths, they probably want to talk all the time! This doesn't mean they should be allowed to. On the contrary, they must learn self-discipline, self-respect, and respect for others. Without these character qualities, paralysis might set in as they're told to be quiet and stop bothering their classmates.

It's usually very effective to allow people-smart children to work with partners and complete projects with small groups. In those settings, they can ask questions, answer questions, and get reactions to their ideas. Another idea that can work for children in all grades is to have them brainstorm with peers for a few minutes as they begin working on their assignment. Then they can return to their seats to work alone. For example, if they're told to begin a creative writing assignment, children with people-smart strengths may struggle with writer's block. Allowing these children a few minutes to talk with others about their preliminary ideas can help them get started.

Because people-smart children are able to read people well, they may also benefit from role-plays, dramas, and demonstrations. They can be a part of these or just watch others complete science experiments and act out, for example, explorers' discoveries.

More than other children, those who are people smart can learn from mentors. Teenagers and adults they look up to can influence their attitudes, character qualities, and ideas. You may also encourage them to shadow people at their jobs to expose them to different careers.

When people-smart children need to write papers on topics of their choice, they might be most motivated when they choose to write about people—inventors, explorers, politicians, Old Testament heroes—rather than places or events. They may also enjoy reading biographies and autobiographies.

Children without people-smart strengths can have this intelligence stretched and improved when they're placed in safe small groups. Choose wisely, though. Expecting them to work with loud, confident brainstormers and quick thinkers might backfire and actually paralyze any people-smart confidence and abilities they were beginning to cultivate. First, they need to gain confidence in sharing and having their ideas critiqued.

You can help children learn to read body language clues and respond appropriately to them by teaching them how you interpret what you do. In other words, if you determined that someone waiting in line with you at the store was worried and not just frustrated, tell your child later how you discerned that. Was it what you heard and/or things you saw? Teach them how you can tell the differences between satisfaction, joy, and eagerness, and between laziness, confusion, and fear.

IDENTITY: WHO AM I?

Because people-smart children like and understand people, they tend to have many friends. If you ask about their day, be prepared to hear about whom they hung out with. They may talk more about whom they had lunch with and what their friends are doing this weekend than what they're learning in their classes. They probably feel most alive when they're with people. It might be hard for children to find the right words to express that, but listen to see if it's implied. You might even come right out and ask them if they think best when they're with people rather than when they're alone. Many people-smart children will be impressed that you discerned that.

People-smart children motivate others, are consensus builders, and peacemakers. They can successfully rally their peers to care about things from class assignments to a special worship concert taking place on Friday night. Better than others, they might be able to plan parties and make decisions about what activities, food, and music would be popular.

Would it surprise you to learn that people-smart children might be great fund-raisers for a school or church project? Think about it. They study people and they're good at reading people. They may be able to determine who might want a subscription to a magazine and who might buy a few candy bars. Moreover, they'll know the best way to ask.

The greatest challenge for most people-smart children is to be without input for any lengthy period. They can most likely handle being alone for a while, but because they think best with others and are most confident of their own ideas when they share with others, they'll struggle if they're alone too much. This may be why they participate in different chat rooms on the Internet and call friends often. They also might reach out to you more often than their siblings might.

Being ignored is also hard for people-smart children. Don't misunderstand me. No one likes being ignored! It's just probably more troublesome for people-smart children.

Struggles

During my student programs on this topic, I usually ask this question: "How many of you have asked your parents a question and gotten them to say yes when you know they should have said no?"

Can you guess the percentage of students who raise their hands? I'd say at least 75 percent! They laugh, and it appears they feel quite proud of themselves. Their mood changes when I say, "Don't ever be proud of that! Shame on you for using a great talent —being able to read people—for evil."

I firmly believe there is a very fine line between our strengths and our sins. People-smart children are great motivators. They can also be great manipulators. Both require the same skill set. Different character qualities and views of people make the difference.

Specific areas of pride people-smart children may struggle with are their people skills and the number of friends they have. They can also develop pride in their ability to manipulate younger brothers and sisters, babysitters, friends, teachers, and you.

PURPOSE: WHY AM I ALIVE?

Showcasing God

God is definitely magnified when people-smart children use their abilities to motivate and encourage people rather than to manipulate them. He is pleased when they help others rather than hurt them; for instance, by welcoming new peers at school and church and by befriending the lonely. They can discern who would be friends with whom and then connect them. They can analyze and improve a group's teamwork and unity. They can comfort others after determining they're sad and give you some space when they discern that you're disappointed. They also showcase God's own character when they enjoy other people's joy.

God is also glorified when people-smart children intentionally use their brainstorming strengths. They can gently help others examine the accuracy of their ideas, consider other people's input when thinking through their own ideas, and think about who would benefit from their ideas, then share them.

As we've seen for each of the other intelligences, God is also honored when children choose to mature in their faith by practicing spiritual disciplines. Because people-smart children think best with others, they'll enjoy the disciplines most when participating with others. They may struggle to worship alone and to learn alone. They will probably prefer to study Scripture in groups. Thus, family devotions may be more important to them than their own quiet time. This, of course, won't be the case if you don't allow them to talk during family devotions. That would frustrate them terribly. Remember, they need to interact with ideas.

Because people-smart children need to talk things through, you'll want to make yourself available to them when they conclude their devotions. Some children may prefer that you come to them and directly ask what they learned that day. Others may want to come to you on their own when they're in the right mood. When you tell them you want to learn from them, they'll most likely take their own study time more seriously.

People-smart children may be drawn to service because they can often discern people's needs. They may know if one of their friends is frustrated, depressed, or angry and what they can do to help. Without directly asking, they may know if a family from the church would prefer meals brought in, groceries so they can cook their own food, or restaurant gift certificates. Because they know many people, they'll know who might help them with their projects. Then they can use their team-building skills to increase the group's cohesiveness, efficiency, and effectiveness.

Evangelism among their peers and family members might come naturally because they study and know people. They may be able to discern who is ready to hear the gospel. They may instinctively know how to turn a conversation to spiritual things, which evangelism approach to use, and which verses and examples to share. They also may efficiently and effectively disciple others to grow in their faith. They may be able to predict what questions people have, what topics to bring up next, which spiritual disciplines will be best, and the like.

Careers

People-smart children will obviously want to consider careers that involve people. I know that my people-smart skills come in handy in my profession as a public speaker, as they did when I taught second graders, coached middle schoolers, and taught university students. Because I'm people smart, I can usually tell if an audience is bored or thinking reflectively. I can tell if I should slow down and allow for more processing time or speed up because people are familiar with the point I'm making. Teachers will be most effective when they develop their people-smart skills.

If your children want to be teachers, you'll be wise to help them hone their people-smart intelligence now. This also applies to many other careers.

Administrators, pastors, and others in positions of leadership benefit from being people smart. Their skills allow them to relate well and connect to people they work with and serve. They understand what people need and can determine how to meet their needs.

Other careers that fit the people-smart profile well include counselors, politicians, lawyers, social workers, evangelists, receptionists, travel agents, advertisers, personnel directors, talk-show hosts, doctors, nurses, consultants, salespeople, police officers, reporters, missionaries, inventors, and waiters and waitresses. Much of their effectiveness will depend on both reading body language and listening to what people say.

I'm blessed with numerous great friends who are multitalented. One of those, George, is an inventor. Because he's heard me teach about multiple intelligences, I asked him which ones he uses when inventing. I had originally thought about listing "inventor" as a career in the logic-smart chapter. Certainly, many people who invent things use skills that could be assigned to the logic-smart category, including George. However, I knew inventing used more than logic intelligence, and I wasn't convinced it was the most significant one.

George told me his invention process begins when he recognizes a need. Once he's done that, he told me, "I talk it through in my own mind." When he is ready, he shares his ideas. He wrote, "I tend to be more people smart than self smart, so I usually work best in a team and bounce ideas off people. As I vocalize the concepts, I tend to understand the next steps. This often occurs before I have finished describing the first steps. Somehow the fact of verbalizing the ideas makes a good connection in my mind, plus it provides the opportunity for people to refine my ideas."

I can so relate to George's process! Maybe you can, too—either for yourself or in the ways you already see your children operate. Do they ever come to you with an idea, but stumble over their words, seeming very unsure of themselves? Wait quietly, listen, perhaps ask a question or two, and restate what you heard them say. They may be trying to think of how to say what they wanted to say at the same time they're trying to grasp the new ideas popping into their minds. It can be confusing! Imagine . . . your children may be people-smart inventors someday!

My brother, who is a clinical chemist and an associate professor of pathology and laboratory medicine, reports that he, too, makes most of his progress when working and talking with others. He knows of people in his field who work mainly alone and are successful. They might even think they're "smarter" because they don't need anyone, but they're not. To expose this myth is just one of many reasons I feel people need to learn about multiple intelligences.

When inventing, George, my brother, I myself, and probably many others begin by seeing a need and spending time alone with our thoughts. During and after this self-smart time, we may activate our word smart to talk to ourselves and make notes. Then, we'll use our people-smart thinking and spend quality time with others. Perhaps we then use our self-smart abilities again and spend time alone with our thoughts, to sift through everything and make decisions. Which other intelligences we use depends upon the ideas or things we're inventing. Everyone has all eight smarts and they work together beautifully!

Ideally, all work teams include people-smart people. Imagine three police officers interviewing people just involved in a traffic accident. The officer with the most people-smart strengths may be the one to determine if someone is lying. Can you think of other implications as you go back over the career list?

BELONGING: WHO WANTS ME?

Most children with people-smart strengths will have many friends. They'll want to spend time with other children, and they may connect at many levels. In order to spend time with others, they may join athletic teams, academic teams such as debate and forensics, work teams such as yearbook and student council, and music groups such as choir and band. They may also be the popular ones who others want to eat lunch with and sit with during sporting events.

As I've cautioned you before, make sure to look for a broad pattern of abilities when deciding if your child has strengths in any of these intelligences. Even if the above paragraph doesn't exactly describe your child, he or she may be very people smart. How is that possible? There are at least two reasons.

First, children can be people smart and introverted. This personality dimension causes children to gravitate toward their inner world. They are quiet, reflective thinkers. Research indicates that their brains even work differently from extroverts.[1] They are fatigued by being with people and energized by being alone. There will be times when their introverted personality type will camouflage their people-smart strengths.

Second, it's possible to have both people-smart and self-smart strengths. As I'll explain more fully in the next chapter, self-smart children think deeply inside of themselves and need quiet and privacy. They don't need people to think with. Therefore, children with strengths in both of these intelligences probably won't have as many friends as children who are much more people smart than they are self smart. Also, if they're both people smart and self smart, and their self-smart intelligence is most activated for a particular reason, it may appear that these children no longer have people-smart strengths. That's not the case.

A pattern I'm aware of is children who behave in very people-smart ways at school, but in self-smart ways at home, where they crave quiet, space, and privacy. Some children have described it like this:

- "I get tired of thinking with and working with kids and need some alone time at home."
- "I get sick of people and need a break before I can be pleasant to my parents."
- "At school I sometimes get tired of being important to people, and at home I'd like to just be ignored for a while."

Is it any wonder that sometimes, during parent-teacher conferences, parents think teachers are talking about someone else's child?

People-smart children usually choose friends wisely. More than others, they'll probably be able to identify who might like them, who they will like, and who will be good for them in one way or another. Other children may seek them out because of their natural leadership gifts and willingness to express compassion. This can result in people-smart children having relationships with hurting and troubled children in need of a confident leader. This will be especially true if people-smart children also have logic-smart strengths. This combination elevates their problem-solving abilities and makes them even more attractive to peers with problems they want solved.

Unfortunately, the same ability people-smart children use to choose friends can also be used for unhealthy purposes. For example, if your people-smart son decides he wants to begin cheating, he might know whom to ask for help. Because he's an excellent observer of people, he probably knows who has been getting away with it. After choosing whom to ask, he'll most likely be able to ask for help in such a way that the other child will say yes. Gang leaders come to mind as a powerful example of this misguided ability. They know whom to target for joining their gang, and they know whom to target for attack. That's why they become leaders. What a sad example of using a strength for evil!

Another potential struggle can arise with children and adults who have something to hide. For example, I've talked with children who are being abused. Because they don't want anyone to know, they've told me about avoiding children and adults who "seem to figure things out on their own."

Connecting with God

Some people-smart children may connect better to Jesus Christ than to God because Jesus seems more identifiable to them. They'll also benefit from learning about God's attributes that relate to interacting with people. For example, they may appreciate knowing that there's no temptation they'll experience that Jesus hasn't (Hebrews 4:15). They'll like knowing that they can love others because God first loved them (1 John 4:19). Because one of their strengths is knowing others, they'll find joy in the truth that God knows them intimately (Isaiah 43:1; Psalm 139; Matthew 6:8; John 10:14).

People-smart children gravitate to group activities where they're allowed to talk and share their ideas. Their other intelligences, personality, and experiences can influence what types of groups fit them best. They may connect well with God at summer camp, youth group, Sunday school, during family devotions, and/or during one-on-one mentoring times. They will get more from worship services and children's church if they know they'll get to share their insights with you after the services. For instance, I know an older teen who listens better to her pastor's sermons ever since her parents told her they'd answer her questions and react to her conclusions every Sunday afternoon. These discussions have provided rich times of bonding.

SECURITY: WHO CAN I TRUST?

Trusting Things

Being able to read people well can feel very powerful. In fact, it can *be* powerful. People-smart children may put their trust in this power and feeling. Their reputation of being good with people and their resulting popularity can also trip them up if they trust these things more than God. On days when they're alone or when they make mistakes with people, they may feel empty and insecure.

Trusting Parents

One of the most important things to remember about people-smart children is that they think best when bouncing ideas back and forth. So to increase their trust in you, talk *with* them rather than *at* them. During these conversations, you can model excellent cause-effect thinking and commonsense reasoning. Ask questions, answer theirs, react to ideas, etc. If they arrive at their own smart conclusions, they'll more likely follow them than if you would have told them the very same thing.

When someone in the family suggests an idea, it's honoring to ask people-smart children, "What do you think?" Of course, your children will need the maturity to understand that what they think won't always influence your thinking. In addition, because they're very plugged in to how others think, it might pay to ask the question, "What would your friends think?"

People-smart children will not trust parents who are hypocrites. I'm not sure other children will either! It's just that children who are people smart are more likely to know when their parents are being hypocritical. You need to remember that your body language is as important as your words. If you say "I love you," but your body language and lack of eye contact indicate disinterest, your child won't know what to believe.

Trusting in God

God is extremely people smart. That's an understatement, isn't it? When people-smart children recognize what they have in common with their Creator, their trust in Him will increase. For example, we see that Jesus related differently to the lost, the Pharisees, and His disciples. He knew what would be best for each type of person. People-smart children are able to do the same thing.

Make sure your children understand that God knows and values them as individuals (see Psalm 27:10; Psalm 139; Isaiah 43:1; John 15:15). Another key truth is that He can be known (e.g., John 10:14–15; John 17:3; Philippians 3:8; 1 John 4:7; 1 John 5:20).

ABILITY AND INTEREST?

Do you and your children have people-smart abilities and interests in common? Using these graphs should help you understand your relationships and past and present experiences. Plotting everyone will also help you decide what to plan for the future.

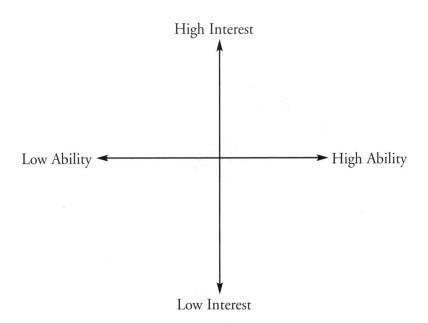

I THINK BY
REFLECTING...
I AM DEVELOPING MY SELF
SMART!

H ey, Carol, I noticed Jake is really quiet. Is he okay?"

"Yeah, Lisa, he's fine. He's just my deep-thinking son who keeps to himself."

"Does he have any friends?"

"He does, but he says he doesn't need them. I know he has fun with them when he's with them, but he's also very content when he's alone."

"I wish Lee was! You've probably noticed that he's my son who can't be alone!"

"Do you know what's interesting? Jake has always been content being alone, even when he was a baby. Now he plays well and studies well alone, too. He tells me he likes thinking about his thoughts. I have a hard time relating to him sometimes! I mean, I have

*thoughts—and some days that's amazing—but I sure don't sit
around thinking about them!"*

"Right! I can't relate well to Jake, either. I'm more like Lee. I like
having people around to do things with and to talk to. I'm not as
comfortable when I'm alone."

"Now that Jake's older, I've noticed something important. When
he does talk, he's worth listening to! Just last night during dinner, all
of us were talking about the different kinds of love. I don't think Jake
said two words until he summarized the bottom-line best. He had
obviously listened well and thought about what each of us was saying. I was impressed with his conclusion. It felt great to affirm him."

Which parent can you most relate to—Jake's or Lee's? Perhaps
your child is like Lee—more people smart. Alternatively, maybe
you're raising a Jake of your own—a child with definite self-smart
strengths. Let's discover what this means.

COMPETENCE: WHAT DO I DO WELL?

Self-smart children think deeply inside of themselves. Therefore,
they can appear to be slow thinkers. Their desire to deeply know
what they know takes time. They don't want to miss any angle of
an issue, and they usually like thinking about their ideas before
speaking up, if they do. More than other children, they may want
to "sleep on their ideas." If you force them to quickly share or if
anyone belittles their "slowness," paralysis may set in. They may
stop reflecting altogether.

Unless this smart is paralyzed by calling them "selfish" because they spend so much time focused on themselves, self-smart
children come to know themselves well. They know their strengths,
weaknesses, what ticks them off, and what calms them down.

They know what interests them, what they don't care about, what they like, what they don't like, what they want, and what they need. They're able to use this self-understanding to guide and enrich their lives. Many self-smart children enjoy reflecting on their past, analyzing the present, and predicting their future. As a result, they tend to be effective goal setters.

Because self-smart children know what they believe and why, they're usually able to stand up for their beliefs. They may become active in a cause, perhaps in a behind-the-scenes role, or they may just talk with friends and peers when the issue comes up in conversation. Their willingness to promote their convictions and opinions will depend, in part, on whether they are also people smart or logic smart. Remember, these intelligences don't work alone. With people-smart and/or logic-smart strengths, self-smart children can convince others their beliefs are right.

Self-smart children tend to be quiet, independent workers and thinkers. In fact, when they're excited, many of them enjoy going off by themselves to enjoy their feelings and thoughts. They don't need others to help them know what they know, and they don't need to tell others what they know. In these ways, self-smart children and people-smart children are opposites.

Learning and Teaching Methods

Some self-smart children may struggle in school because teachers ask for their answers and opinions, which they'd rather keep to themselves. These children need to be willing to play the game of school—to answer teachers' questions even if doing so doesn't enhance their own understanding. Although highly self-smart children are satisfied knowing what they know, and it's not important to them that others know, you can encourage them to participate in class and completely answer their teachers' questions. If they don't, their grades may not always reflect their true knowledge or abilities. It goes beyond that, however. Self-smart children often have excellent insights because of their deep-and-wide thinking. If self-smart children can realize how much others may benefit, it will build their confidence and motivate them to stretch beyond their comfort zone by expressing their thoughts.

Children regularly are required to share their ideas with others. They're called on in classroom discussions, they must share group work in school, and respond when you ask questions about what they're studying. All of this stresses self-smart children. Because these children prefer to study alone, your desire to interact with them can create conflict. Everybody's "interference" (a word some self-smart children use when I talk with them) can make school and learning very stressful for them.

Grading is often unpleasant for self-smart children because it involves the evaluation of ideas. Providing an answer key for the first few problems of an assignment helps some students. When these children get immediate feedback and see how they're doing, they gain momentum and concentration to complete the assignment.

Since self-smart children are quiet and find it difficult to talk with their teachers, their teachers may not know them well. Nevertheless, it's crucial that they do! I've found that teachers may judge self-smart children harshly just because they don't understand them. This is where you can step in as your child's advocate. You may need to help teachers understand your child's self-smart strengths and the difficulties they sometimes cause.

It may take self-smart children longer to collect their thoughts and respond to a discussion question than other children. Teachers can give them time to process their ideas. They can let children know they'll call on them fourth at the beginning of tomorrow's class, after Kevin, etc. These types of considerations honor children and increase their confidence. This, in turn, facilitates a smoother class discussion.

As much as possible, connect topics to these children's personal lives because that's how they think—by relating learning to their lives. You can look over their homework and help them discover how the topics are relevant and how they might be relevant in the future. They may balk at participating in activities they believe have no personal benefit. In school and in life, they may ask, "What does this have to do with me?"

Self-smart children like choices and options. These can be simple—write in cursive or print, do the first or second set of ten problems, and read a biography or mystery for their next book report. Of course, being given a choice is a privilege. If they complain about their options or take too long to decide, tell them they've lost the privilege. Then tell them specifically what to do.

Self-smart children will also benefit from individualized instruction and assignments they can complete independently. You also motivate them by creating opportunities to engage their feelings.

Children who *don't* have much self-smart strength may need other people's input in order to think well. These children will often want (or even need) to share their conclusions with you and/or their siblings, teachers, and peers. Providing questions for them to reflect upon and answer privately may help them develop their self-smart thinking abilities. Whereas self-smart thinkers know what questions to ask themselves, those who are just developing this strength will need guidance. You can begin by providing them with numerous questions, then fewer, and gradually expect them to think of their own. When they reflect privately on their conclusions, they can learn to savor the joy of knowing. Learning to rest in our own thoughts can be challenging, but so beneficial.

IDENTITY: WHO AM I?

Since knowing themselves well is a strength of self-smart children, if you ask them to describe themselves, you may be listening for a while. On the other hand, since it's not important to them that others know them (unless they're also people smart), they may not share much at all. If this is the case, it's easy to conclude that your child is insecure and quiet.

Self-smart children may describe themselves as loners, thinkers, quiet, aware, and careful. They may admit to liking privacy, quiet, space, and time. They may tell you they *need* it. As I've cautioned you before, make sure you look for broad patterns that indicate children have this intelligence strength before you assume they do. For example, children who are introverted by personality may say they're loners. Children who have been neglected, abused, or hurt emotionally may behave like loners. This doesn't necessarily mean, however, that they're self smart. In other words, they don't think deeply and privately, and they don't automatically relate learning to their lives.

Because self-smart children have a hard time separating themselves from their ideas, they may tell you a lot about what they believe when you just want to hear about how they are. This difficulty with separating themselves from their ideas is why being evaluated stresses them so. Much of their identity is wrapped up in what they know. When what they know is evaluated, they feel evaluated as a person. It's one and the same. Through your parenting and affirmations of their entire identity, you can help them believe they are more than their ideas.

Self-smart children might admit to being bored or angry when their time is wasted. They can also feel frustrated when they want to think deeply about something that no one else seems to care about. Many have told me it's awkward if they want to think about something when others want to have fun. They don't want to be a downer, and they're sometimes made to feel that they are. This may be doubly true if they also have logic-smart strengths.

Struggles

Self-smart children can be very independent and are often content being alone. Therefore, they can become self-centered. Some develop an "It's all about me!" attitude to life.

Pride in their own ideas and in their ability to explain their ideas are possible sins self-smart children need to guard against. They can also believe their ideas are more important than anyone else's. These are tendencies of logic-smart children, too, so if your self-smart child is also quite logic smart, it's especially important to watch for, talk about, and pray against these tendencies.

Self-smart children admit they can struggle to remain open to other people's ideas. Their self-knowledge and deep thinking causes them to be satisfied with what they know. Moreover, until they have time to think about other ideas, whether from pastors, parents, teachers, or in textbooks, they tend to be skeptical. Some have admitted to being unteachable. Others tell me they're not, but they admit to often behaving as if they are. (Until hearing my school assemblies, chapels, or church youth-group programs, these self-smart children didn't understand where their lack of teachability was rooted. My instruction helps them discover their intelligence strengths and accompanying sin issues. This empowers many of them to feel less guilty and to choose to change. I'm thankful!)

Many self-smart children value self-discipline. They develop high standards for themselves. When they make mistakes or "mess up," they can be very hard on themselves. Being critical, coupled with being alone and not seeking other people's input, can result in hopelessness and fear.

PURPOSE: WHY AM I ALIVE?

Showcasing God

How do self-smart children glorify God, or put Him on display? One way is by being true to themselves. Because they know themselves well, self-smart children are able to be who God created them to be. God is glorified when any of us behaves as He designed us to.

Self-smart children tend to know their natural abilities, spiritual gifts, personality, and preferences. Through faith in Christ, they come to understand that these abilities weren't given to them to please themselves, but to serve others. This is one of the greatest advantages of self-smart children who trust Christ. It helps them move beyond themselves, to take interest in and feel concern for others. God is glorified when self-smart children use their identified talents, intelligences, and skills to bless others.

As with the other intelligences, how self-smart children practice spiritual disciplines will depend, in part, on their spiritual maturity. They may struggle with several spiritual disciplines if they're made to feel they must be practiced corporately. For example, they may be prayer warriors in private, but not feel comfortable praying in public. That's okay.

Self-smart children may worship God well in private. Because they can go deep within themselves, they may be able to enter into His presence during a worship service better than most. They may be able to block out distractions and concentrate on what they want to communicate to God and what He is saying to them.

They may prefer studying Scripture and spiritual books during quiet times rather than in family devotions. However, they'll struggle to have their own devotions if they can't find Scriptures and/or books they can relate to. Self-smart children may enjoy journaling their thoughts and prayers. The disciplines of silence and meditation will also appeal to them. They can often easily apply what they learn to their lives.

Because self-smart children think deeply and are aware of their thoughts, feelings, and actions, they don't hide from their sin. They glorify God through confession and repentance. In this way, they're good for the whole church. Especially if these children also have people-smart strengths, they can also serve God by motivating others and being their accountability partners.

Careers

Perhaps you've been thinking about what careers would appeal to self-smart children. If you thought of things they can do alone, that's a sensible conclusion. However, depending on other intelligence strengths, they may want to relate to people during at least part of their day or week. For instance, they may be interested in sales or research because they can be on their own during most of the week, but they can also interact with others as they need to.

Being self-employed and doing something they have great passion for may be an excellent fit. They'll need to have enough people-smart skills to understand how to sell their product or motivate people to be interested in their ideas. Self-smart children may turn out to be successful entrepreneurs. They may start a company, turn it over to others, and go start another company. They might work with crafts or drama. They might become private investigators, poets, or writers.

Because they're in touch with their own thoughts and feelings, they may be able to help others get in touch with theirs. Like people-smart children, they may become excellent pastors, counselors, social workers, teachers, and therapists. They'll need to be confident and secure in order to be successful. Because they enjoy thinking about the future, they may want to consider becoming guidance counselors. A personal trainer may also be a good fit.

BELONGING: WHO WANTS ME?

Many self-smart children appear to be shy and quiet, especially when they're in crowds or with a new group of peers. As a result, it may appear that they don't need to be wanted. That's not true, though, as every person is born with a need to fit in and connect with others. It's just not as pronounced for self-smart children.

The self-smart intelligence can be paralyzed when children constantly hear feedback such as, "Get your head out of that book," "You're being selfish again," "Don't you have anyone to play with?" or "You're such a loner!" Children may begin to believe these negative comments.

Self-smart children think of themselves and their own ideas before they think of others. They also like being alone. They tell me that family and friends voice concerns and, as a result, they often feel guilty. Just a few weeks ago, when speaking at a conference hosted by a large Christian school, I saw several posters with this traditional saying: "JOY—Jesus, Others, Yourself." This, and other Christian messages, can make things uncomfortable for those with self-smart strengths. They can't *not* put themselves first. They're self smart, not necessarily selfish or prideful.

Most self-smart children are probably most comfortable hanging out with one or just a few friends at a time. They may prefer friends who are like them—quiet and reflective. I know some self-smart children who enjoy spending short amounts of time with vibrant people-smart peers because the contrast is energizing.

Self-smart children may meet their need for belonging through individual sports and activities they can do alone, yet while in a group. Cross-country, tennis, and swimming are sports that may appeal more to self-smart children than sports like volleyball, basketball, and football. Being a photographer for the yearbook and being in charge of posting flyers for the youth retreat may also be appealing.

Because children who are self smart know themselves well, they usually don't make foolish mistakes. This quality can be very attractive to children who make mistakes or are unclear about what life is all about. Self-smart children can help others discern their strengths and challenges. They can also help them set sensible goals and make plans to reach them. This input will help to awaken and increase the self-smart intelligence.

Since self-smart children know what they know and they prefer to think carefully about ideas, they can usually stand up to peer pressure. This is another strength that might attract some peers.

How might self-smart children struggle in relationships? The word *intensity* comes to mind. They might not feel safe and comfortable with lots of intense energy from people-smart peers or those who are outgoing and extroverted, regardless of their intelligence strengths. The intense, deep thinking of self-smart children may turn off their peers.

Also, remember that self-smart children want to relate topics to their lives. If they're with a group or their family and they can't relate to the topic being discussed, they may disengage. Perhaps you've seen this happen. These are the children who are physically present but mentally absent.

Connecting with God

Based on conversations I've had with confident self-smart children, I think many children with self-smart strengths have deep connections with God. You may not know this about your own self-smart children, since they're not motivated to share much. Their relationship with God may be very private. If your children don't talk about Him, don't assume He is not important to them. Remember to look for patterns. If your self-smart children are quiet about many relationships, and you struggle to know much about their friends, it shouldn't surprise you if they treat their connection to God in similar ways. You can hope that, at the right time, when the mood and reasons are right, your self-smart children will talk about God with you. You may want to try journaling back and forth because this method will appear to be more private and less intrusive than conversations. You'll need to be vulnerable and transparent for the journaling to be successful. This should eventually lead to face-to-face enjoyable conversations.

Self-smart children probably connect well to God by reflecting privately on what they hear about Him (e.g., 2 Timothy 2:7). This might be why your son or daughter doesn't join the family discussion in the car on the way home from church. Self-smart children pay attention during church services, midweek programs, Sunday school, and family devotions, and then go off by themselves to reflect on their initial thoughts. That's their power —reflection and the knowing that comes from it (e.g., Psalm 63:6; Psalm 105:5; Psalm 119:27).

Self-smart children may reflect while lying on the bed, mowing the lawn, making their bed, organizing their collections, or jogging at the track. Reflection often leads to self-examination. This and the repentance, forgiveness, joy, and gratitude that follows is often used by God to deepen their connection.

SECURITY: WHO CAN I TRUST?

Trusting Things

Unfortunately, like children with other intelligence strengths, self-smart children can be tempted to place their trust in things. Their own ideas can be so important to them that they begin trusting in them. The totality of their knowledge and their self-understanding are other sources of security for self-smart children.

And what about their independence? Self-smart children may trust too much in their ability to handle things alone. They sometimes define themselves by their privacy, quiet, space, and secrets. Although there's nothing wrong in being independent, it's possible to cross the line to depending on it. It would be unhealthy for self-smart children to believe they were successful because they were independent.

Trusting Parents

If you want your self-smart children to trust you, you need to know them. This can be challenging because they don't necessarily share a lot. Nevertheless, it's essential. You'll make more progress when your input fits them well. So pay attention to them. Watch and listen. Interact as you can. Let them know you want to talk and be available when they might be in the mood to talk. This might include while you're running errands, because they can talk without needing to make eye contact, and as you put them to bed, because the dark often makes it easier to bring up significant issues.

You'll also want to give them time to reflect, think, and feel before, during, and after discussions about important topics like discipline, motivation, homework, and faith. Valuing their thoughts, and telling them you do, is very important.

Asking your children for their thoughts and recommendations also honors them. Again, just like with people-smart children, self-smart children need the maturity to understand that you don't need to accept all their suggestions. You will listen and work to understand their perspective. This, of course, needs to go both ways. If you listen respectfully to your children's conclusions and recommendations, they need to listen to yours.

Trusting in God

Self-smart children benefit from knowing that God knows their thoughts (e.g., Psalm 139:4; Matthew 9:4). Although it's not important to them that *you* know their thoughts, I encourage you to do what you can to engage them in conversations about spiritual things. You can help them be sure of their forgiveness, and you can determine if they have major doubts or questions.

I believe personal testimonies can reach self-smart children. They may pay close attention to these during church services, Christian school chapels, children's church, and youth group. They'll learn by trying to put themselves into the speakers' shoes. It might be even more beneficial when you invite people into your home to enjoy a meal with you. As they share what God, Jesus, and the Holy Spirit means to them, your self-smart child will be pondering and learning. In the safety of your family, your child may be willing to ask important follow-up questions. Because you know your child well, you might also ask your guests to share what you know will be helpful for your child to hear. These guests can be missionaries, pastors, and teachers. They can also be other church members, people in your neighborhood, work colleagues—anyone who might enrich your child's life.

ABILITY AND INTEREST?

To assist you in drawing accurate conclusions about the self-smart interests and abilities of each member of your family, take the time to complete these graphs. Keep in mind what you've observed in the past and what you learned here.

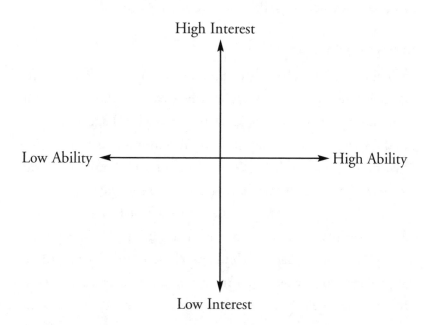

High Interest

Low Ability ← → High Ability

Low Interest

THE COMBINATION OF PEOPLE-SMART AND SELF-SMART STRENGTHS

Take a minute and flip back to the graph you completed at the end of the people-smart chapter (chapter nine). Compare that graph to this one. Did you rate anyone in your family as high ability in both people smart and self smart? If you did, that person may live in an almost constant state of internal stress and confusion. He or she has perhaps been accused of being moody and in need of counseling! (This certainly isn't true of everyone with this combination of strengths. Mature, healthy people can learn to shift between these two strengths, as appropriate. It's not easy for children, although they tell me that understanding these two smarts helps them tremendously.)

I often explain it this way: People who have both people-smart and self-smart strengths may be the life of the party on a Friday night. The people-smart intelligence was activated and taking the lead. They connected to most of the people. They were able to help some people have a better time by determining their mood, discerning what could change it, and then following through. They had a genuinely great time and said they'd be back the next Friday night.

One week later, they felt obligated to go to the party even though they weren't really in the mood. Maybe they heard something on the radio, were asked a question by a teacher or coworker, or read a Bible verse that activated their self-smart thinking. They would have preferred to stay home where it was quiet and where they'd have space and privacy. Instead, however, they went to the party. Rather than being the life of the party, they stood by themselves and didn't really connect to anyone.

Soon after arriving, a friend approached:

"Are you okay? You're so quiet."

"Yeah, I'm fine."

Ten minutes later, the same person asks, "Are you sure you're okay? You can talk with me, you know."

"I'm fine. Don't worry about it."

Ten minutes later, the same person stops by again. "Have I upset you or something? You seem distant."

"I told you I'm fine! Just leave me alone!"

Is it any wonder that people with high people-smart and self-smart abilities confuse themselves and others? They're equally skilled at bouncing ideas off others and thinking deeply within themselves. They know themselves well and they know others well, too. They're comfortable with people and alone. Therefore, at times they don't know where to go or who to be!

When I teach high school students about this internal conflict, many cry and thank me for helping them understand themselves. They tell me they've thought they were crazy or sick. They tell me about many conflicts with friends, parents, and siblings who complain they're inconsistent and hard to figure out.

In the middle of my explanation of this phenomenon, some teens have actually shouted out, "That's my mother!" Then others laugh and point to themselves to indicate they think they have at least one parent with this double strength.

In one-on-one conversations, teens tell me they've thought they were the problem. I've heard about how they come home from school and their mom wants to hear all about their day. Then the next day, they're greeted with, "Not now. Can't you find something to do?" I help them understand that several things can cause these different reactions, including high people-smart and self-smart intelligences. These teens are relieved to learn that it's not necessarily true that they've done something to anger their mom. They're empowered to now give their parents some space if they discern they're in self-smart mode and engage them in conversations when they determine their people-smart skills are ruling. How freeing!

CONCLUSION

Did you find valuable golden nuggets as you dug into the multiple intelligences? I sure hope so! Maybe you found some good-sized gems. I hope you regularly paused to praise God for generously creating you and every child with many smarts. Maybe you thought about how He is smarter than us and how that's something to be very grateful for, too. Like me, are you also grateful and humbled by the fact that He equips us and trusts us to serve Him?

I hope the graphs at the end of each smart chapter were helpful. If you look back at them and see that you consistently rated one or more of your children as high ability *and* high interest, I encourage you to ask yourself whether those evaluations indicate unfair expectations or pride. They may not, but I think it's worth asking the question. Of course, looking at where you rated yourself on all eight graphs is also a good idea.

On the other hand, if most of your ratings for one child were in the low-ability *and* low-interest quadrant, perhaps you have developed a critical spirit toward him or her. That may not be the case, especially if the child is still very young. Nevertheless, you just may want to go to God with your evaluations and ask Him to show you if you've been fair. You also may want to ask Him to show you if any of the intelligences might have unwittingly been paralyzed by you or others. Ask God to open your eyes to which intelligences might need to be reawakened and to opportunities to do so.

MORE RESOURCES

I invite you to go to our Web site:

www.CelebrateKids.com

Click on the image of the book and you'll discover helpful resources. You can download as many graphs as you want so you can create new ones as your children's interests and abilities shift. In addition, I strongly encourage you to list all eight smarts on one graph for each person. These will be beautiful summaries of each person and of your entire family. You can update these, too, as you apply new ideas and strengthen the intelligences. For example, here's how my intelligence profile looks at the time I'm finishing the book:

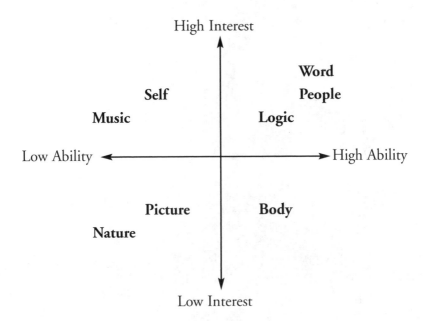

I've also included other evaluation systems that are fun to do with children. On the Web site, you'll find bar graphs, pie graphs, and additional information, including answers to frequently asked questions, that you can use to focus and train your children's smarts. Please check it out!

Everyone associated with Celebrate Kids, Inc., believes each of your children is a unique, one-of-a-kind, unrepeatable, never-to-be-seen-again miracle. When you provide beneficial nurturing, give them the freedom to be who God created them to be, and teach them to embrace self-control, self-respect, and respect for others, they can be very successful.

From my heart to yours: Always celebrate your children for who they are and not just for what they do. May you and your children be smart with your smarts! To God be the glory!

Great books from Dr. Kathy Koch

Celebrate Kids, Inc., is a non-profit organization dedicated to helping parents, educators, and children of all ages meet their core needs of security, identity, belonging, purpose, and competence in healthy ways. Through a problem-solving framework of these integrated needs, our programs and products provide

solution-focused strategies that improve their intellectual, emotional, social, physical, and spiritual health.

FREQUENTLY ASKED
QUESTIONS

Q. *Is there a test I can give my children to determine how much of each intelligence they have?*

A. There's no test that Dr. Howard Gardner, the "father" of the theory of multiple intelligences, endorses. Therefore, for me, the answer to this question is no.

The use of one test to assess all eight would violate the model because children would have to use their word-smart and logic-smart intelligences to take the test. I suppose several independent "tests" could be created for each of the eight smarts so all facets of each smart could be analyzed. Would it be worth it, though? It would take a lot of time and energy to take and score these assessments.

I agree with Howard Gardner, who is against testing for

fear that new forms of labeling and stigmatization might result. Rather than using these smarts as a way of categorizing individuals, we should emphasize their use in learning and studying so more children are academically successful.

Q. *In addition to the line graphs, are there other charts we can use to evaluate our children's intelligence strengths?*

A. Yes. Please go to www.CelebrateKids.com and click on the image of the book to find additional charts you may download.

Q. *Is there the possibility of other intelligences being discovered?*

A. Howard Gardner has written about the possibility of an existential intelligence as recently as 2006. He still labels it as provisional. He defines this intelligence as an "ability to contemplate phenomena or questions beyond sensory data, such as the infinite and infinitesimal."[1] Whether this or other strengths qualify as intelligences according to his strict criteria remains to be seen.

Q. *Are strengths in the multiple intelligences influenced by gender or culture?*

A. They may be, but since there's no formal assessment to score people on, it's impossible to know for sure if one gender or people group is stronger than another. I, again, concur with Dr. Gardner. The danger in thinking that there might be differences between groups is the labeling and judging that would take place. Also, I believe that some differences we assume are due to intelligences may be due to learning styles, personality, and spiritual gifts instead. I have spoken of this idea, however: It appears that picture-smart people would find Asian languages (e.g., Chinese, Korean) easier to learn than those who are not very picture smart. This does not necessarily mean, however, that more Asians are picture-smart than people from another race.

Q. *Are there certain children's books that might be fun to use when activating or strengthening our children's smarts?*

A. Yes. So I can keep the list current and add some recommended by readers, you'll find this list posted at www.CelebrateKids.com. Just click on the image of the book.

Q. *My children are teenagers and beginning to date. Is knowing about their smarts relevant?*

A. Definitely. After helping them identify their intelligence strengths, you could brainstorm with them to determine how these could be a blessing in a relationship. For example, if your daughter is very nature smart, she might want to ask her boyfriend if they could talk while walking in a park instead of while just sitting in a restaurant. Knowing your son is picture smart could help him think of new things to do with his date. And, of course, if he can predict her strengths, he'll come up with suggestions to honor her. It's also valuable to discuss how someone could use your children's intelligence strengths against them. For example, if a boyfriend knows your daughter is word smart (he might not call it that—he might just realize she responds well to words) then he might know he can sweet talk her into doing something she really doesn't want to do. And, if your son is body smart and thinks through touch and movement, and his girlfriend figures this out, she may use physical contact to wear down his defenses. As thinking while dating is essential, work with your children to come up with other scenarios. In general, we teach the pre-teens and teens in our prevention programs to not drain their brain when they start their heart.

Other practical questions, similar to the one above, are posted at www.CelebrateKids.com. Clicking on the image of the book on the home page will get you there. If you have a question that isn't answered there, please e-mail it to me at questions@ CelebrateKids.com. I can't promise you a personal response, but my staff and I will post answers to the questions we think are relevant to many.

NOTES

Chapter 1: "How Am I Smart?"
An Introduction To Multiple Intelligences

1. Except for my family and coworkers at Celebrate Kids, Inc., all names have been changed.

2. If you're interested in knowing Dr. Gardner's criteria for categorizing something as an "intelligence" versus a skill or talent, please see his 1993 book, *Frames of Mind: The Theory of Multiple Intelligences* Tenth-Anniversary Edition (London: Fontana Press), 62–67.

3. H. Gardner, "Reflections on Multiple Intelligences: Myths and Messages," *Phi Delta Kappan* 77 no. 3 (1995): 203.

4. In most places in this book, I use "children" to represent children and teenagers of all ages. When an idea or example is relevant just to teens, I'll make that clear by using "teens." If something relates only to young children, I'll make that clear, as well.

Chapter 2: What Are My Core Needs?
How Are Multiple Intelligences Relevant?

1. For a complete and practical explanation of these five core needs, I encourage you to read my first book: *Finding Authentic Hope and Wholeness: 5 Questions That Will Change Your Life* (Chicago: Moody, 2005).

2. J. Walters and H. Gardner, "The Crystallizing Experience: Discovery of an Intellectual Gift," quoted in *Conceptions of Giftedness*, ed. R. Sternberg and J. Davidson (New York: Cambridge Univ., 1986).

3. Thomas Armstrong, *Multiple Intelligences in the Classroom*, 2nd ed. (Alexandria, VA: Association for Supervision and Curriculum Development, 2000).

4. Ibid.

5. Correcting children well isn't easy—it's a fine art. My CD "Fabulous Feedback: Complimenting and Correcting Children" offers practical help that's relevant to adult relationships, too. You can order it on our Web site: www.CelebrateKids.com.

6. I cover the dangers of perfectionism in my first book, *Finding Authentic Hope and Wholeness*. I encourage you to read it if this is a relevant concern for you and/or your children.

Chapter 3: I Think With Words . . .
I Am Developing My Word Smart!

1. Dr. Tom Armstrong includes a lengthy list of professions for each of the eight intelligences in his book *You're Smarter Than You Think: A Kid's Guide to Multiple Intelligences* (Minneapolis: Free Spirit, 2003). In *Seven Kinds of Smarts: Identifying and Developing Your Multiple Intelligences* (New York: Penguin, 1999), he includes a list of job skills along with the list of professions.

Chapter 9: I Think with People . . .
I Am Developing My People Smart!

1. For a fascinating discussion on how the brains of introverts and extroverts differ, see *The Introvert Advantage: How to Thrive in an Extrovert World* by Marti Olsen Laney, Psy.D (New York: Workman, 2002). Laney also discusses how the term "introvert" is misused and misunderstood, and gives strategies for introverts to recast introversion as a strength and use it to full advantage.

Frequently Asked Questions

1. Moran, S., Kornhaber, M., & Gardner, H. (2006). Orchestrating Multiple Intelligences. Educational Leadership, 64 (1), 25.

INDEX